Praise for F

"As ancient Israel tells it, Pharaon, with his ~~~~~~ ~titude, speed, and control, is over and done with. Except that, as these wise authors know, Pharaoh continues to reappear in new forms. These alert and discerning authors—one a Christian and one a Jew—see that Pharaoh's mode or leadership has too long dominated both church and synagogue with the practice of top-down, all-knowing, all-controlling leadership. By teasing out the biblical text and citing compelling contemporary embodiments, these authors advocate and celebrate an alternative form of leadership in religious communities that is marked by openness, collegiality, and forward-anticipating restlessness. This is practical theology at its best. The book is a primer for how to bring our leadership practices into sync with our core tale of emancipation. The model of Moses both permits and requires our departure from Pharaoh and his leadership. These authors know how and where to look for such a generative alternative."

—Walter Brueggemann,
Columbia Theological Seminary

"Never more needed, this book is a gift to all who read it and a gift to the world when its readers live into its message. This book is half faith-based wisdom literature, half management-science handbook for transformation in a turbulent age, and 100 percent visionary map to loving and leading more creatively and more effectively."

—Rabbi Brad Hirschfield, president,
National Jewish Center for Learning and Leadership

"*Picking Up the Pieces* is a revelation. Elegantly written and warm as a cup of coffee, it is the heart-gift of two friends, faith leaders writing for all of us with flocks to lead. McShane and Babchuck can't help themselves—they are playful and provocative preachers, looping us into a journey that they themselves are on. But make no mistake: this book boldly rewrites the script that frames pastoral ministry. You'll see your leadership with new eyes after you read these pages. For me, it was just in time."

—**Kenda Creasy Dean**, Mary D. Synnott Professor
of Youth, Church, and Culture, Princeton
Theological Seminary, and author of
*Almost Christian: What the Faith of
Our Teenagers Is Telling the American
Church* and *Innovating for Love:
Joining God's Expedition through
Christian Social Innovation*

"Any time a rabbi and a Methodist minister get together on a project, you can expect something special. But this book is something extra-special: to-the-heart, wicked smart, and right-on-time wisdom for ministers, rabbis, and leaders of all shapes and sizes. We could wish this book on every religious leader, every seminarian, and every leader engaged in vital change-making work."

—**Brian D. McLaren**, author of *Faith after Doubt*

"*Picking Up the Pieces* challenges the reader to examine long-held assumptions about vision, power, control, and effective leadership. A compelling read that weaves Scripture, midrash, and case study—making an artful argument for a different leadership model in a new era."

—**Susan Beaumont**, consultant and author
of *How to Lead When You Don't Know
Where You're Going: Leading in
a Liminal Season*

more human—the people of God, leaders in a new story. May it be so."

—**Rev. Lisa Greenwood**, president and
CEO, Wesleyan Impact Partners and
Texas Methodist Foundation

"Kathleen McShane and Elan Babchuck offer a vivid and memorable parable for a leader's journey—reminding us that the difficult road from boss and functionary to enabler and inspirer requires interior travel too. The road eases with growing distance from entrenched power and with more travelers showing the way."

—**Matthew Barzun**, author of *The Power of Giving Away Power: How the Best Leaders Learn to Let Go* and former United States ambassador to the United Kingdom

"Read this book slowly. Wisdom is more often not a new idea but, rather, a careful, nuanced study of familiar things in a radically different way. Kathi McShane and Elan Babchuck have done a remarkable job offering wisdom about leadership by revisiting texts and leaders to show us something importantly different—and actually sustainable. Slow down and capture this necessary gift."

—**Gil Rendle**, minister, consultant, teacher, and author of *Countercultural: Subversive Resistance and the Neighborhood Congregation*

"Babchuck and McShane have designed a must-read text for effective faith-rooted leadership. *Picking Up the Pieces* is steeped in extensive exegesis, interfaith wisdom, vulnerable life lessons, and applicable practices for leading in a more empathetic and holistic way. They don't just flatten the traditional hierarchical leadership model of a pyramid; they blow it wide open so that the voices of all of God's beloved children are heard, honored, and woven into God's ongoing love story with creation."

—**Rev. Dr. Victoria Atkinson White**, managing director,
Leadership Education at Duke Divinity and author
of *Holy Friendships: Nurturing Relationships
That Sustain Pastors and Leaders*

"*Picking Up the Pieces* is an invitation to a life of leadership marked by trust and mutuality, with a shared vision of power that is at home in God's world and God's generous way of being. The remarkably instructive and human approach to Moses's leadership transformation, along with stories from life-giving contemporary leaders, combine to paint a picture of a way of being that is profoundly livable for leaders and deeply honoring of the gifts within communities. This book can both nourish the soul and provide actionable pathways for life-bringing leadership. Leaders who allow themselves to be shaped in these ways will find the promise of joy and flourishing, right in the midst of the always-profound challenges of leadership."

—**Dr. Aaron Kuecker**, president,
Trinity Christian College

"With Rev. Kathi McShane and Rabbi Elan Babchuck we have two authentic voices melding their honest, hard-earned reflections with lessons gleaned from others who learned to lead from love, not power. They are charting a path toward the only kind of leadership that offers the prospect of continual renewal in this post-empire period—leadership that helps others come fully alive to their potential, living with curiosity and love in the tension of humble uncertainty."

—**Anne Evans**, leadership group member,
Ashoka Innovators for the Public

"To say this is a timely, innovative, and even essential book is to miss its greater message. Our cracked and crumbled maps, models, and guides are in pieces all around us. Through personal experience, insightful engagement with holy texts, and stories of co-journeyers, Kathleen and Elan invite us into the journey of Mosaic leadership, picking up the pieces of the world as it is so that we can co-create the not- yet of the world that is to come."

—**Rev. Steve Lawler**, founding director,
Walker Leadership Institute,
Eden Theological Seminary

"What a relief to remember that religion has been reimagined before, and what a joy to see where it might be going. McShane and Babchuck's insights on leadership and interpretation of tradition nourish the spirit and stimulate the imagination. When you're ready to relinquish control, this book is the perfect dance partner."

—**Casper ter Kuile**, author of *The Power of Ritual: Turning Everyday Activities into Soulful Practices* and cofounder of Sacred Design Lab

Picking Up the Pieces

PICKING UP THE PIECES

Leadership after Empire

Kathleen McShane   Elan Babchuck

Fortress Press
Minneapolis

PICKING UP THE PIECES
Leadership after Empire

Unless otherwise cited, Hebrew Bible quotations are from *The Holy Scriptures: A New Translation* (Jewish Public Society, 1917) in the public domain. Accessed at https://www.sefaria.org.

Unless otherwise cited, New Testament Scripture quotations are from *The Common English Bible*. Used by permission. All rights reserved.

Kei Miller, "Book of Genesis," from *There Is an Anger That Moves* (2007). Printed with the permission of Carcanet Press Ltd and the poet.

Rodger Kamenetz, "The Broken Tablets," from *The Lowercase Jew*. Copyright 2003 by Rodger Kamenetz. Published 2003 by TriQuarterly Books/Northwestern University Press. All rights reserved.

Gregory Orr, "Not to Make Loss Beautiful," from *Concerning the Book That Is the Body of the Beloved*. Copyright © 2005 by Gregory Orr. Reprinted with the permission of The Permissions Company, LLC, on behalf of Copper Canyon Press, www.coppercanyonpress.org.

Library of Congress Cataloging-in-Publication Data

Names: McShane, Kathleen, author. | Babchuck, Elan, author.
Title: Picking up the pieces : leadership after empire / Kathleen McShane, Elan Babchuck.
Description: Minneapolis : Fortress Press, [2024] | Includes bibliographical references.
Identifiers: LCCN 2023023005 (print) | LCCN 2023023006 (ebook) | ISBN 9781506490977 (print) | ISBN 9781506490984 (ebook)
Subjects: LCSH: Christian leadership.
Classification: LCC BV652.1 .M434 2024 (print) | LCC BV652.1 (ebook) | DDC 262/.1—dc23/eng/20230821
LC record available at https://lccn.loc.gov/2023023005
LC ebook record available at https://lccn.loc.gov/2023023006

Cover image: Scenic View of Mountains against Sky in Egypt - stock photo ©Anastasiâ Lis / EyeEm | Getty Images
Cover design: Kristin Miller

Print ISBN: 978-1-5064-9097-7
eBook ISBN: 978-1-5064-9098-4

Elan

For Lizzie—my wife, my partner, and my teacher. You have taught me a lifetime of lessons about patient grace and generosity of spirit—sometimes through your words, always through your ways.

And for our children, Micah, Nessa, and Ayla—this mysterious, messy, miraculous world will soon be yours to shape. Trust yourselves, love your neighbors, and listen for the still, small voices you'll encounter along your way.

Kathi

For changemakers everywhere—may God take your heart and set it—keep it—on fire.

Together

And finally, we dedicate this book to each other. To have discovered in each other a teacher is a precious gift; a friend is a treasure. But to have found a kindred spirit who responds "Yes!" before you can even finish sharing an outlandish idea is a pearl of infinitely great value.

Contents

PROLOGUE

Listen
Suppose there was a book full of only the word,
let—from whose clipped sound all things begin: fir
and firmament, feather, the first whale—and suppose

we could scroll through its pages every day
to find and pronounce a Let meant only for us—
we would stumble through the streets with open books,

eyes crossed from too much reading; we would speak
in auto-rhyme, the world would echo itself—and still
we'd continue in rounds, saying let and let and let

until even silent dreams had been allowed.

— KEI MILLER, "BOOK OF GENESIS"

Let is a risk-taking verb. To *let* something happen is quite different from *making* something happen. To invite whatever a *letting* brings is to relinquish the control we imagine we have, trusting that whatever may come—fir, firmament, feather, the first whale, as the poet imagines—will be good. The Genesis story begins with a Creator who says, "Let there be." Let there be light, landscape, life. As if there were already partners to whom the Creator's vision could confidently be entrusted. As if whatever happened next would be pleasing, no matter what form it might take in its coming to be.

This is God's story.

This is not the story we have been taught about what leadership means, what it does.

This book is about unlearning the lessons of leadership gleaned from a culture obsessed with control and certitude. It's about acknowledging the cost of a leadership born in the pyramids of the Egyptian empire, one that suppresses the spirits of its leaders *and* the people who follow them. It's about the corrosive effect of addressing people, and being addressed, in commands that begin with "do this," never "let." In these pages lies an invitation to lead in a different way. That invitation is embedded in another biblical story, about Moses, who had to unlearn the empire's model of leadership before eventually learning a different way from the One who began with "Let . . ." Moses's story begins with a promise of liberation and ends on the doorstep to a promised land. And so does ours.

We, this book's authors, are a baby boomer United Methodist pastor who founded a small movement that is rethinking the work of the church, and a millennial rabbi who leads a think tank and founded a network for spiritual entrepreneurs.[1] We met in April 2018 at a small gathering of hopeful, faith-based innovators. Kathi had just begun as the senior pastor of a large church in Silicon Valley and already felt the undertow of decline under her feet. Elan had recently left a position serving a large synagogue in Providence, Rhode Island, and was beginning to discern the contours of a calling that might nurture both his faith and his entrepreneurial spirit.

From Kathi

For most of the years I was a pastor, what I felt most acutely was my responsibility for the well-being (or maybe the survival) of the churches and organizations I led. I'd grown to think of my calling as leadership—of the local church I was officially responsible for and the denominational institution I had committed myself to. I was frequently frustrated with a church that seemed focused on its own preservation. Its bureaucracies felt clunky, resistant to change; they were the opposite of nimble. What consumed our attention was the viability of our own institutions, not the spirit that was meant to flow through them. The tides of our daily work pulled us further and further away from the liberating invitation to step into the current of inclusive love that is the essential message of Christianity.

In 2017, the Silicon Valley church I led embarked on an experiment. What would happen, we asked, if we combined the compassion of Jesus that's demonstrated in the Gospels with the practical skills of social entrepreneurs? What if we reimagined discipleship as becoming compassion-driven changemakers like Jesus? Our questions and a one-year partnership with the social entrepreneurship organization Ashoka led to the Changemaker Initiative and a fledgling movement of changemaker churches across the United States.[2]

Our theory was that the church could be reinvigorated, not by some ambitious strategic plan but by laypeople encouraged to be agents of transformation in the workplaces, schools, and neighborhoods where they were already engaged. Imagining an empowered cadre of change agents sounded to me like an echo of Jesus's Great Commission, when Jesus dispatched the disciples to go out and replicate his message without the benefit of a syllabus or style guide. Jesus must have known each of those followers would speak truth differently, filtered through their own experience. There was no chief disciple charged with maintaining a centralized vision. Jesus trusted the Spirit's presence in the hearts and minds of every follower. His faith rested in the whole arc of God's vision—that what goes wrong will be made right, even without immediate intervention. That vision yielded the first-century church, described in Acts, a church that seems to have thrived without a centrally managed structure.

The early church was a loose, lacy fabric of faithful people connected by the movement of an unpredictable, unfettered Spirit. The church tried new things and no doubt failed more often than we know. But it also flourished because it invited people's active, creative engagement rather than their subscription to a plan that was already fixed in place.

The changemaker work turned my understanding of ministry on its head. Reimagining Jesus as a compassion-driven changemaker prompted a new understanding of Christian discipleship, one with less focus on what happens in church and more on what happens in the everyday lives of laypeople, whose attention is and always was focused mostly outside the organization (let's be honest). I came to realize that their inclination to be more interested in their work or school or family than they are in the institutional concerns of their church isn't a distraction; it's their calling. Listening for and encouraging those callings is the church's work. It was also my work as a pastor. My core responsibility shifted from safeguarding the institution to equipping and blessing actions inspired by the loves, the commitments, and the work that real people do in real life—all of which happens in settings *outside* the one I was in charge of. That meant I had to think about my leadership differently.

This shift required me to consciously distribute the power that came with my position as the public leader of a faith community. I had to practice what did not always come intuitively: a more daring trust that others—laypeople, staff members, less senior colleagues—would feel as compelled to join God's work in the world as I felt. I had to hold my decisions more lightly and to expect that challenges from others might lead us in a better direction.

It was the hardest, messiest work I had ever done. My leadership experiment failed as often as it succeeded in accomplishing what I intended. I have no doubt my colleagues and congregants sometimes wondered whether I knew what I was doing. As we pushed through two-plus years of a pandemic and significant uncertainty about what the church's new normal would look like, my less commanding direction sometimes disappointed the people who expected me to be more directive than I felt called to be. But people grew into deeper faith, more active engagement. Our relationships changed; we became partners and friends. And the church's ministry expanded into places I imagine God had long been waiting for us to show up.

From Elan

When Kathi and I met, I was in a liminal moment of life, straddling two worlds and desperate to bridge the gap between. I had recently departed a position serving a relatively healthy, large synagogue in New England, where I worked (overworked, if we're being honest) with a remarkable team of staff, clergy, and laypeople to revitalize the congregation with innovative new programs and engagement efforts. We grew rapidly during that period through a mix of new affinity groups, a bold business model that centered on financial transparency, and community-organizing work that brought new life to our justice work in the neighborhood and beyond.

To be clear, the success was far from overnight. We worked day and night, seeking out new leaders in the unlikeliest of places and inviting them to take ownership of their community. Our goal was that our community members would no longer belong to our temple; we wanted our temple to belong to them. But even as we celebrated small wins along the way, I started noticing a marked restlessness in many community members. All the change was exciting (if a little destabilizing), but there was still an underlying nostalgia for a world that was already long gone. I would watch as some of our longtime members would walk into the sanctuary, and as they made their way to their regular seats, they would linger for just a few extra moments at the empty seats that—in their mind's eye—were once regularly occupied. I listened to the concern of board members who, in spite of their appreciation for the young folks joining the community, wondered aloud during board meetings why the "youngsters" weren't coming to prayer services. And even when they did, they certainly didn't know any of the classic melodies.

Underneath the growth and excitement was a deep and persistent sense of loss—a yearning for a world that once was, a yearning that often manifested as a resistance to the world that was coming into being. Nostalgia never had a vote at our board meetings, but it always had a veto. Meanwhile, I, too, was growing restless and, to be fair, exhausted. My wife and I had just welcomed our second child, Nessa, into the world. Between the sleepless newborn nights and the endless working days, I found myself pulled between the congregation's expectation that I would stay with them for a lifetime and my own nostalgia—not for a world since passed but for one yet to be. A nostalgia for the future.

I felt a deep hunger to take what I had learned at the synagogue, marry it with my earlier experiences building start-ups, and share those insights with others like me, people I came to think of as spiritual entrepreneurs. I could sense that what I was experiencing was by no means an anomaly. There were countless others like me committed to building models of faith for the future that married the best of where we'd been with the highest aspirations of where we might go. And by the time I announced my departure and my impending move to join Clal - the National Jewish Center for Learning and Leadership,[3] the shape of what would later become Glean Network, an incubator for faith-rooted leaders, began coming into focus.

Two years and two cohorts of spiritual entrepreneurs later, I sat two seats over from a remarkably impressive, courageous pastor who spoke of a transformation underway at her church on the other side of the country. She shared vulnerably about the challenges of stepping out of her power to create space for others and simultaneously about the joy of witnessing those emerging leaders bring new ministries into being right there inside her church. When the session was over, I raced over to Kathi to introduce myself, and we've been in holy conversation ever since.

Kathi and I left our first meeting with an emerging friendship and a new vision of leadership in our own contexts that would alter the trajectory of our work and our lives. After just a few hours of honest, faithful conversation, we both had a creeping sense that a new story was unfolding before us. It was a story that spoke to our personal experiences—our past failures, our grief about the unraveling of religious life in America, and our frustrations with the institutions we served, meant to serve people created in the image of God but built in the image of the empire. More than we knew in that moment, each of us was feeling our way toward a vision that could hold our hopes for the future, stitched together from the threads unraveling from today's religious life and tomorrow's, too. We surely didn't know that our experiences of breaking in and breaking with the institutions we'd served would inform a new vision of what faithful leadership looks like.

There is another voice in this book too: Moses's. It is said that there has never been another leader like Moses.[4] Chances are, you are not another Moses. Surely we, this book's authors, are not. But the truth is, neither was he. Much of our modern understanding of Moses as an individual, a prophet, and a leader is shaped by mythical exaggerations about his life. From early midrash to later biblical commentaries to recent books such as *Moses on Management: 50 Leadership Lessons from the Greatest Manager of All Time*,[5] Moses's story has been stretched, mined, and rewritten countless times to yield a version of him as the platonic ideal of a leader.

What most of those elegies leave out is that Moses was not always an exemplary leader. He was most certainly not born one. Moses became a great leader. In the stories of the exodus, we watch him learn in the same way we learn most of the important lessons of our lives: by stepping forward, stumbling backwards, and then pushing ahead once again. Moses spiraled his way into wisdom, letting its lessons sink in deeper as he circled back to discover them once, twice, then again.

The exodus narrative suggests that Moses's growth occasionally came through flashes of revelation, but more often it emerged through gradual recognitions that seeped in over long stretches of time. Sometimes he was moved by soulful insight, sometimes by the voice of God, and sometimes it was an irksome member of his tribe who called him to attend to a blind spot. Often, a new way of being came with the message, "You can't do it that way anymore. It's not working." In the process, Moses's intermittent uncertainty about how to lead the unruly flock he'd been assigned was as intense and uncomfortable as ours sometimes feels.

Exodus is not only the story of a physical journey; it's a journal of internal transformation. Forty years of leading an obstinate people through a treacherous wilderness changed Moses. He learned, gradually, to trust his congregation as partners in the shared project of liberation. And the people changed too. They gathered agency along the way, power to listen for and respond to God's calling all on their own. They learned over the course of their journey to modulate their voices, from complaint to contribution. They discovered that obedience and resistance were not the only two options available to them.

The pace of Moses's and the people's mutual transformation— his becoming an empowering leader, their becoming an empowered people—was not always evenly matched. Sometimes Moses dragged the Israelites toward unrealized potential; sometimes they surprised him, claiming an inspiration he hadn't yet felt. But regardless of who initiated each step, Moses and his people eventually found, over the course of their breakneck escape from slavery and their excruciatingly slow passage through the wilderness, that the shape of their relationship was shifting. As Moses was tested and transformed, he unlearned the patterns of coercive power he'd absorbed growing up in Pharaoh's palace. As he released the singular authority he thought leadership both gave and required of him, the people rose to their potential as partners. When the promised land finally came into sight, it was a light in all of their eyes.

This is our journey, and it is the journey of every leader who dares to step toward a more expansive vision. We are molded by the humbling experiences that loosen our grip on power, on certainty, on control—all those things that once seemed necessary to scaffold our seats at the top of pyramid-shaped structures. The passage will be daunting. But its end is liberation.

Notes

1 Technically speaking, Elan is actually a "geriatric millennial."
2 www.thechangemakerinitiative.org.
3 Founded in 1974 by Elie Wiesel and Rabbi Yitz Greenberg, the National Jewish Center for Learning and Leadership (Clal) is a think tank, leadership-training institute, and resource center. Bringing Jewish insights to a wide American audience, Clal makes Jewish wisdom an accessible public resource. A leader in religious pluralism, Clal builds bridges across communities, and promotes participation in American civic and spiritual life, reinvigorating communities and enhancing leadership development.
4 "Never again did there arise in Israel a prophet like Moses" (Deut 34:10).
5 David Baron, *Moses on Management: 50 Leadership Lessons from the Greatest Manager of All Time* (New York: Atria, 1999).

Introduction

Richard Rohr writes, "We all come to wisdom at the major price of both our innocence and our control."[1] If he's right (and we think he is), the first quarter of the twenty-first century has been a colossal wisdom-generating exercise for all of us, especially for leaders of religious organizations. Our eyes were already trained nervously on the horizon. For decades, we had watched the slow fade of Americans' bond to the institutions that had once shaped them. And then came the Covid-19 pandemic, and with it the loss of any notion that we could steer clear of disruption. A few technologically astute and highly adaptive faith institutions thrived, but for most of them, the slow decline of prior decades accelerated toward free fall.

Even as we have shifted into a post-Covid world (if such a world exists), today's religious leaders continue to find themselves sequestered in a wilderness governed largely by disorder and scarcity. Everywhere we look, what is most apparent is what we lack. We see the world not for what it is, nor for what it might yet become, but for what it used to be. We know that we are losing our footing, but the landscape is shifting too quickly to discern whether it is the ground that is slipping or us.

For three years, we (Elan and Kathi) have worked together designing and facilitating an annual four-week clergy intensive—a sort of boot camp for pastors who are trying to reinvigorate their congregations. We ask: What would happen if you were less focused on the tasks necessary to maintain your congregation's familiar, regular routines? What if you spent your time and energy and the power that comes with your position making your organization more pliable, more open to the unexpected, more willing to bear the risks that accompany change? Again and again, we have heard from those clergy leaders a deep yearning: to break free from the weight of their daily, status quo–sustaining tasks. And we can feel their sheer exhaustion.

They say things like: "It takes all the energy I have just to keep the train running on the track, let alone on time." "I'm tired. I've tried everything to turn my congregation around; I just can't do any more." "I just don't have the charisma that successful church pastors must have." It takes extraordinary effort and an unreasonably broad range of skills to lead a congregation these days. One has to be both a generalist and a specialist at all times, swapping hats across an ever-widening range of roles. If it ever was, it is no longer enough to visit the sick and preach a good sermon. Most clergy leaders feel as if they are barely hanging on to the responsibility they're entrusted with, racing as fast as they can to close the gap between a fixed tradition and a culture that is steadily drifting in the other direction.

If we stretch ourselves to our limits, we can *almost* keep up with serving both the entrenched and the disenchanted, the deeply invested and the utterly disinterested. If we are exceptionally energetic, we *might* make a few marginal improvements on the bundle of traditions that has been delivered into our hands. We wish we could be more innovative. But to shift resources toward creating something new requires a relinquishment of the control and certainty that our traditional organizations suggest as a promise—to leaders and congregants both.

The clergy intensive course is an exercise in rapid reorientation. Pastors are asked to reconsider their role and the sense of fulfillment they derive (or not) from directing (and sometimes controlling) the scope and scale of their congregation's ministries. They're invited to experiment with loosening their hold on a clearly defined position at the top, to see what it feels like to share power with even the unlikeliest of their congregants.

This book grew out of the honest, vulnerable discussions among those brave pastors who dared to question the expectations that have traditionally rewarded their work as institutional leaders. They are endeavoring to pick up the pieces of a world that once seemed solid and unassailable and to put them back together into a mosaic whose outline is unpatterned, still emerging. In writing this book, we're picking up those pieces too. And in reading it, so are you.

Surveying the Landscape

This book is divided into three parts, each representing a critical juncture in Moses's leadership journey and the Israelites' liberation from slavery. Along the way, you'll meet six remarkable contemporary leaders—Reverend Eugene Kim, Rabbi Adam Kligfeld, Rabbi Sara Luria, Reverend Maurice Winley, De'Amon Harges, and Father Richard Springer—who embody many of the countercultural leadership traits that constitute Mosaic leadership. Before, between, and after each part, a "logue" will punctuate the text—a prologue, two interlogues, and an epilogue. Each of these sections offers a meditation on a particular moment in the life of Moses. His transitions are illustrations of this checkered journey: stumbling, dusting himself off, moving forward again, a little wiser.

Part 1 introduces one of the most potent forces in Moses's story and ours: the pyramids. In the biblical tradition and in today's organizational landscape, pyramids symbolize security, certainty, and unshakable stability. They are omnipresent, standing in the imaginations of those who built them, those who inhabit them, and those who live in their shadow.

Chapter 1, "The Pull of the Pyramids," explores why the pyramid shape is so persistently attractive in organizational life and how an empire built in their image remains so sturdy all these centuries later. Chapter 2, "Cracks in the Façade," presents the myriad downsides to institutions built in the model of the pyramids and their corrosive effect on people, on purpose, and (ironically) even on productivity. Chapter 3, "Breaking Free," offers a curated history of relevant leadership theories that have risen to prominence and sometimes faded from it quickly. Calls for a more generous model of leadership have been persistent but drowned out by the prevailing theory of the day. These offerings—the prominent theories and the calls for a better alternative—might still serve us today, if they can be rearranged to serve in today's tectonically shifted leadership landscape. And finally, in chapter 4, "The Way Up Is Down," there are stories of breaking—with tradition, with our institutions, with our old ways of leading. These stories mirror the percussion that sounded when Moses dropped and shattered the first set of stone tablets at the foot of Mount Sinai. As Rebbe Nachman of Breslov wisely instructs, "If you believe that it is possible to break, believe that it is possible to repair" (Likutey Moharan 2:112).

Part 2 introduces the idea of Mosaic leadership, a model of leadership shaped by the wilderness and marked by a willingness to share power with others. As with Moses's journey, a Mosaic leader must first choose to depart from the way things used to be and then learn how to lead generously and gracefully through the wilderness, where our most significant leadership challenges await. Chapter 5, "What We Leave Behind," documents what vestiges from the past are no longer useful and must be abandoned—for the Israelites who left Egypt and for today's leaders who have set their sights on a different path forward. Chapter 6, "Liberating Structures," proposes that organizational structures are powerful tools for adjusting organizational culture, and even ad hoc adjustments can have long-term impact. It offers a number of practices to build a healthier culture without completely disrupting the existing structure. Chapter 7, "Testing for Trust," expands on the idea that God moves at the speed of our relationships. Offering, expecting, and earning more trust will create the kinds of organizations that are well-suited for the wilderness and will change the leaders who guide them. Chapter 8, "Power Struggles," explores the unique challenges of leaders who dare to lead counterculturally. This is not easy work.

Part 3 offers a summation of wisdom learned and offers practices for the road ahead. The path of Mosaic leaders has no singular course but rather is navigated by essential practices that help leaders calibrate their compass along the way. Chapter 9, "Mosaic Leadership," introduces seven core practices of Mosaic leaders, based on lessons gleaned from Moses's life, our experiences, and the stories of the six exemplary leaders you'll meet in these pages. Building on those practices, chapter 10, "Are We There Yet?," outlines the three-part Mosaic leadership cycle: dreaming, disturbing, and distancing. The cycle—a virtuous one, we propose—is continuous. It invites you to draw the courage you need to thoughtfully examine your current state and prepare for the next stage in your leadership life.

This book is framed by the story of Moses's journey through the exodus and the often-overlooked narrative of his evolution as a leader. We look to this story not only as the scriptural text of our religious traditions but in the spirit of *Sankofa*. Sankofa is a symbol that comes from the tradition of Akan storytelling centered in the West African nation of Ghana. The mythical Sankofa bird flies forward while it looks back to where it has already been. Literally, the word means, "It is not wrong to go back and pick up what you have forgotten."[2] The exodus is the larger, foundational story that makes meaning of every journey from bondage to promise. It lodges the long wilderness in between those two poles inside God's perennial promise of liberation. Sankofa summons our attention with the same hope of freedom to mine an exquisitely human story of a leader whose transformational struggles parallel our own.

Each chapter includes a Sanfoka frame—a story of Moses's leadership that wraps around the contemporary picture taking shape in the chapter. The frames adhere closely to the biblical narrative of the Israelites' exodus from slavery and the evolutionary transformation of their leader. Think of them like signal lights, directing our exodus experience toward a whole and redemptive narrative.

Just like those of the clergy in the twenty-first century, Moses's inherited ideas about leadership had to be deconstructed to make room for new possibilities. For him and for us, the process is uncomfortable, disorienting, and occasionally painful. That's what it means to move through the wilderness. In a close and unusually personal reading of Moses's transformation, in his leadership epiphanies and the errors alike, and in the repeated assertions of agency from the people "below" him, we find a glimpse of what we might call *Mosaic leadership.*

Leadership is Mosaic in its reflection of the life of Moses himself, this leader like whom there is no other (Deut 34:10). It becomes Mosaic as it adheres more closely to generosity, patience, human dignity, and a deeply rooted humility—values that have little currency in the leadership patterns formed by empire. It takes on Mosaic significance as it acknowledges the truth that faithful leadership is glued together out of broken pieces, shards of the expectations that empire culture has burdened us with carrying forward.

We—you—are still the holders of an ancient promise of liberation. When people enter and offer themselves to a community of faith, they're seeking to be a part of something greater than themselves. They're begging for a hint of the flourishing that God intends for every living being. It's time for leaders to take their entreaties seriously, to experiment with a model of leadership that worries less about the size of their congregation and more about the size of each person's impact among that mixed multitude.

This book is an invitation and a challenge to religious leaders and organizations to step into Mosaic leadership—an experiment in consciously moving out of the penthouse at the top of your organization's pyramid—so that a collection of people can lead together. This exercise will require risking an order that our organizations have come to depend on. Success might feel fleeting, more like a staccato drumbeat than a consistent chorus. But maintaining a status quo that refuses to welcome the fullness of every contribution poses a far greater risk in the long run.

Walter Brueggemann calls us again and again to the perspective that the biblical story is a counternarrative to what the culture has taught us to believe in, to trust, to shape our personal and organizational lives around. The contours of Mosaic leadership are messy and imprecise. It's no wonder that tracing them can feel agonizingly slow and sometimes counterintuitive. But isn't this precisely how God's work among us looks?

Notes

1   Richard Rohr, *The Universal Christ: How a Forgotten Reality Can Change Everything We See, Hope For, and Believe* (New York: Convergent Books, 2019), 247–48.
2   The Spirituals Project at the University of Denver, "African Tradition, Proverbs, and Sankofa," https://tinyurl.com/yxh2x4cw.

Part I

Disturbing the World as It Is

CHAPTER ONE

The Pull of the Pyramids

Passover Prep: Elan's Story

I come from a family that never made too much fuss about birthdays or holidays. We didn't decorate the house with balloons and streamers. We didn't swim in Hanukkah gifts for eight straight nights. For the most part, the bells and whistles of our get-togethers were the people; most of my childhood memories involve a house full of dear friends and extended family, often gathered around the piano while my father played the blues and we all sang along. But Passover was the one exception. Passover at the Babchuck house was an event.

One year, my father made a full-size poster, with words and accompanying pictures, of our favorite song, "Echad Mi Yodea" ("Who Knows One?").[1] When it came time to sing it, my Grandma Etta jumped out of her seat, ruler in hand, and mimed the whole song while we broke out in laughter. Another year, our family friend Andy hid the *afikomen* inside the VCR,[2] and all of us kids looked frantically around the house for a full hour until he finally gave up the hiding spot. And (while I don't have the clearest memory of this) there was one year that I mistakenly drank Manischewitz instead of grape juice, and— despite months of preparation—could not remember even one of the Four Questions when called on to recite them.[3]

It wasn't just the laughter that framed those Passover memories. The themes—breaking out of narrow places to discover new freedoms, making home wherever we found ourselves in the world, and connecting across generations through storytelling—all mattered deeply to our family. Both of my parents were far from home, geographically for my mother and existentially for my father. Stories of home allowed them to create a new narrative and build a new life together. And they never missed an opportunity to share those stories with me, my brother, and my sister.

So we treated Passover like the most important holiday of the year. For several weeks leading up to it, I'd listen to my parents negotiating menu plans, coming up with engaging ideas for the Seder,[4] and checking in with guests about any specific needs they might have. As the holiday approached, the energy level would tick up a notch each day; all five of us were tasked with swapping out dishes, cleaning the house, and preparing for our respective leadership roles in the Seder.

Once the floors were swept, the kitchen wiped spotless, and countless boxes trucked in and out of various closets around the house, my favorite part of Passover prep took place: setting the table. As the youngest in the family, I appreciated the responsibility of playing social engineer, imagining which pairs of guests would make for interesting conversation. And once the place settings were established, then came the best part: the decorations.

I don't know where it originated, but we had this antique brass set of stacking pyramids, and we would polish them each year before the holiday until they shone majestically. All through the Seder, I would fidget with them, stacking and unstacking them, arranging them in different patterns, and wondering whether they looked anything like the real thing. In my eyes, these pyramids were perfect: symmetrical, sturdy little structures that represented not only the hard work of my distant ancestors but also the staying power of the mortar that held them together. All these years later, after wars and storms and earthquakes and floods, after civilizations rose and fell and rose again, the pyramids still stood strong.

So around my tenth birthday, when my mother shared the news that in our upcoming trip to her homeland of Israel we would be taking a detour to Egypt to see the pyramids and would even be allowed to go into the Pyramid of Menkaure, I nearly lost my mind. There wasn't a place in the world that I wanted to visit more than Egypt, and we would soon be on our way! In my mind's eye, I pictured standing at the foot of pyramids, larger than any building I could imagine, touching the bricks with my own hands, connecting with history in a way I never thought possible. But as I would later come to learn, when it comes to pyramids, there is a wide gap between real and ideal.

Pyramids Everywhere

What Elan's ten-year-old self didn't yet know is that pyramids aren't found only in ancient Egypt; they're all around us. Today they are the model for many—maybe most—organizations. The same structures that once promised unalterable stability to the ancient Egyptians are now occupied by employees, volunteers, and members of countless institutions all around the world. Thousands of years after Egyptian pharaohs commanded construction of brick-and-mortar pyramids to house their wealth, we are still building up organizational structures that cut the same triangular outline into the horizon.

Today, pyramids serve as monuments to institutional life; they shape our reality. Buildings, systems, clubs, and academies are mostly formed in their image. Leadership operates from the apex; operations are supported by a wide base. The shape preserves a consistent and predictable order. Our position within the structure tells us precisely what our power is and who holds power over us. The original pyramids symbolized an unshakable empire. Scripture teaches that our ancestors once gave shape to them; today, the roles have reversed. Those pyramids now give shape to us, for better and, as we will explore in these chapters, for much, much worse.

Follow the Leader

For as long as humans have walked the earth, we have stratified into leaders and followers. Human nature drives us to form tribes and teams, and for good reason: few tasks can be accomplished without cooperation. Someone must lead; others must follow. But how do we know who is a worthy leader and who among us is prepared to follow?

Enter the triangle. While it is rarely found in the natural world, this is the shape we most commonly use to organize ourselves. Throughout human history, in fact, the triangle has described, and in some cases prescribed, the constellation of human relationships. From family trees to organizational charts, the Star of David to the Holy Trinity, civilizations throughout history have relied on the triangle to give order to the disordered and often messy relationships that hold us together. Want to know who's in charge? Just look up.

In the language of religious traditions, we strive to reflect the divine image, to replicate what the Creator once did, to take the *tohu va'vohu* (formlessness; Gen 1:2) of life and reorganize things until they seem "good" in our eyes. But our earnest attempts to live into this divine function—making order out of chaos—have grown so stiff as to completely stifle their life-affirming origins.

Christian theology understands a triangle—the Trinity—as its most essential element. If the triangle is God's arrangement rather than a mark of limited human imagination, it is surely there to align with nature's own cycles, to reflect a fluid dance among three mutually dependent partners.[5] But in our human hands, over the course of thousands of years and a parade of powerful empires, the triangle has been transformed. One individual rises to the top of the triangle, sequestered, omnipotent; everyone else finds a less significant place below. As centuries have passed and human interactions have gotten more complex, the shape has been stamped on our families, our communities, and even our informal associations. The organizational leaders Ann Linnea and Christina Baldwin observe in *The Circle Way*:

> The triangle is the basic unit of family (father/mother/child); the triangle divides how we see ourselves (body/mind/ spirit); the triangle shapes how we view society (church/ state/individual). . . . Looking at the triangle as a system of socialization, we get powerful leaders located at the top and followers, employees, and ordinary citizens located at the bottom, with gradations of authority assigned and maintained in a status-based worldview.[6]

It's impossible to pinpoint precisely when the triangle ceased to be descriptive—an attempt to neatly approximate how humans related to one another—and became prescriptive instead. Perhaps it was when the very first three-sided outline was scratched into a cave wall, right next to the first circle. Maybe our Paleolithic ancestors chose between the two shapes and preferred the sharp lines of the triangle to the difficult-to-replicate circle. Maybe it was as the earliest tribes first yielded to the alpha in the group. Or maybe it was when the biblical Egyptian pharaoh saw that his influence could be extended, like his empire, through an architectural innovation that translated a triangle into a three-dimensioned monolith.

Regardless of when the shift actually occurred, the result is clear: a triangle is no longer just a triangle. It symbolizes a system that elevates a few and confines all the rest. It's a pyramid: a triangle that defines the structure that leaders climb and then narrowly outlines the point from which they exercise power.

Empire: Cementing the Path of Power

Beginning in roughly 1550 BCE, the Egyptian empire dominated Middle Eastern culture, knowledge, technology, and sophistication, advancing each in such profound ways that they continue to shape our world today. Architects of their empire's advancements, Egypt's pharaohs were elevated into gods whose power was believed to rival all others (most notably the God of Israel). When they died, the pharaohs' bones were gathered into the pyramids—eternal monuments to their leadership. At the time, these pyramids were the most imposing structures in existence, visible from miles away, standing tall over the flat desert dunes. They symbolized wealth, power, and divinity, and they conveyed such to everyone who laid eyes on them.

Those pyramids cast a long shadow. Several thousand years after their construction, from thousands of miles away, we still live under the pyramids' influence and the empire they represent. The theologian, biblical scholar, and contemporary prophet Walter Brueggemann repeatedly calls our attention to the features of contemporary life that replicate Egypt's command of its people's attention, loyalty, and service. Brueggemann's insight and scholarship make empire a metaphor for power that commands from the top, a domination unseen but obeyed, a counterforce to the compassionate, justice-seeking character of the God of Israel.

Brueggemann notes the marks of empire evident in Egypt and still visible among us in contemporary life:

- Affluence far beyond mere satiation. This is opposite to the hunger that forced the Israelites into dependence on a daily provision of manna. A glut of products turns humans into consumers and tamps down the revolution of freedom and justice that signals the ongoing work of God's creation.
- Oppressive social policy, exemplified in the extreme by forced labor, but evident wherever human dignity is

disregarded. The grind of the economy's engine, its constant need for the fuel of our efforts, eclipses our impulse toward compassion and justice.

- Static religion, in which the sovereignty—the freedom—of God is encased and constrained. In empire, the purposes of power—whether administered by pharaoh or the king, the state or the institution—are paramount. Those purposes claim and mobilize the energies of the people. Consciously and unconsciously, the practices of religion bend to those purposes.[7]

Empire subversively establishes culture, even now. We are deeply immersed in it, but we lack awareness of its hold, the indisputable narrative it has put in place. This culture sets our expectations about what is normal, what operates this way simply because that's the way things are. Inside the contours of empire, Brueggemann says, "religion is to be an opiate so that no one discerns misery alive in the heart of God. Pharaoh, the passive king . . . in the land without revolution or change or history or promise or hope, is the model king for a world that never changes from generation to generation. That same fixed, closed universe is what every king yearns for—even Solomon in all his splendor."[8]

The Empire's Seductions

Is Brueggemann correct in his assessment that every king—perhaps even every leader—is subject to the empire's seductions? In the stories of the biblical tradition, it is God who chooses and elevates Israel's tribal leaders and kings—Moses, Joshua, David, the prophets. They were called into service; God appointed them to a top spot. Sometimes God insisted on their suitability over their protests of inadequacy and built scaffolding underneath their flaws. Moses was not a natural public speaker. David was a hedonist. Jeremiah was clearly too young. God anointed them one by one into positions of power and in doing so gave them the singular authority to direct others into action.

But God did not override their humanity. Their genius often charted the nation's path to greatness, but sometimes their failures in management led the whole country astray. The biblical narrative suggests that a leader's personal sinfulness can shape the fate of a whole people: David's dalliances, the excesses of Solomon's sons. When the sovereign is unfaithful, the kingdom's character, and the divine safety provided to it, erodes. The Hebrew Scriptures tell this story with fable-like clarity. A corrupt leader can dis-integrate a large-scale enterprise, a whole country.

This is the power of a leader who sits at the top of any pyramid-like structure: to set the course for the entire assembly below. Bertrand Russell famously said that power is, simply, the ability to make things happen, even over resistance.[9] The proverb holds true on a small scale too. In every community—families, neighborhoods, congregations—power is present even when we are not aware of it; it informs virtually every human relationship. Andy Crouch, in his book *Playing God*, observes, "Like the electric current that runs, with the rarest of interruptions, through my home, power is a fundamental feature of life. And as with electricity, those who have the most unfettered access to power are the ones who are likely to think about it the least."[10] Those with reliable access don't think about electricity until there's a blackout. The same holds true for those with access to the power that fuels our organizations.

The Architecture of Religious Empire

As pyramid governance grew more popular with each passing civilization, it gave shape to the many ways that those civilizations organized themselves. From politics, to the economy, to educational systems, pyramid-shaped architecture has framed and preserved the many building blocks that make up modern society. Religious organizations are no exception. Today denominational authority commonly rests with a single executive, a pope, an archbishop, or occasionally a small council. Power filters down through carefully monitored channels, losing potency at every layer of the arrangement. Finally, only the thinnest remnant of authority arrives at the ground floor—which is, in the world of religious hierarchy, often the unordained laity. Their enlistment in and financial support of the enterprise is critical, but their decision-making, direction-setting power—their ability to make things happen—is nominal.

Despite the many benefits they provide (stability, clarity, order), pyramids are not places where liberation and agency—the lifeblood of a civilization's beating heart—flow freely. In fact, as Elan came to learn during his long-anticipated childhood trip to the pyramids, they were just the opposite.

Revisiting the Pyramids: Elan's Story Continued

I grew up in a crowded town in the Northeast with precious little space to roam, so any encounter with a sweeping, stretching landscape was memorable for me. After several days of traveling in cramped planes, buses, and taxis, the camel ride to the deserts of Giza felt otherworldly. Not only was I soon to encounter the ancient pyramids that I had long dreamed of, but I was surrounded on all sides by sheer, rolling expanse.

From the time we caught sight of the pyramids until our camels finally plodded to a stop felt like eternity. Every few minutes one of our camels would stray from the line, stubbornly refusing its rider's pleas until the pleasures of disobedience subsided and it rejoined the group. So what should have been an hourlong ride through the desert took several hours to complete. When we finally arrived, we dismounted, handed the reins to our tour guide, and waited in line with our tickets in hand. As the line inched forward and I approached the third pyramid, I squinted against the sunlight to take in its full shape. Just like the brass miniature on the Seder table, this pyramid cut perfect lines in the sky, a magnificent triangle atop a pristine sea of sand. It was breathtaking.

When our turn to enter came, I could barely contain my excitement. I braced myself to behold the tombs of ancient pharaohs, the luxurious adornments of gold and precious gems throughout—just like I had seen in documentaries. I imagined cavernous chambers inside to match the monstrous footprint of the structure.

When the security guard took our tickets, he encouraged us to take one last, deep breath of fresh air and to enjoy it, because it was the last one we'd enjoy for quite some time. And he was right. It struck me instantly that—even at ten years old and on the low end of the height chart—it felt eerily like the walls were closing in on me. The further into the pyramid I got, the more my breath felt labored, constricted. I broke out in sweat from heat, to be sure, but even more so from anxiety. The tunnel was not only pitch black, with oxygen at a premium, but somehow it felt hotter than it did outside in the midday sun. Expansive this was not.

And once our group shuffled into the first room, another disappointment awaited us. Between the early graverobbers and the modern plunderers who had visited over the past four millennia, the pyramids had been stripped completely bare. So while I certainly appreciated the chambers' relative spaciousness compared to the tunnels, the destination surely didn't justify the journey.

For all their staying power, the pyramids weren't all they were made out to be, at least not the idealized version that my ten-year-old mind had conjured over years of building them up. Of course not. The pyramids were not designed for life to flow through them—in fact, just the opposite is true: they house immobility. And the same holds true for the organizational pyramids that the empire has tasked us with toiling over, building and rebuilding them, year after tireless year.

▲

Born in the Shadow of the Pyramids:
Moses's Story

Moses was born into an empire, too. The giant sandstone pyramids that dominated the landscape molded his expectations about what leadership looks like. God's call to Moses at Horeb over the specter of a burning bush was dramatic, life altering. But the call did not wipe clean the inscribed slate of Moses's lived experience. At birth, he was fixed by ethnic origin into a category of people who could imagine no way out of slavery. Adoption into Pharaoh's household catapulted him into a social structure more free but no less confining, the household of a sovereign whose authority was never questioned. Moses saw firsthand, and then traversed uncomfortably, the gap between two hedged enclosures, one at the top of the pyramid and the other at the bottom.

Generations before, the Israelites, descendants and relatives of the biblical Joseph, had come to Egypt as invited guests. They were ready to work, eager to contribute, even celebrated in their accomplishments. Their enthusiasm may have seemed like bounty at first, but as generations passed on, it occurred to the Egyptians that the sheer size of their collective presence might hold a threat.

A new king arose over Egypt who did not know Joseph. And he said to his people, "Look, the Israelite people are much too numerous for us. Let us deal shrewdly with them, so that they

may not increase; otherwise in the event of war they may join
our enemies in fighting against us and rise from the ground."
    So they set taskmasters over them to oppress them with
forced labor; and they built garrison cities for Pharaoh: Pithom
and Raamses. But the more they were oppressed, the more
they increased and spread out, so that the [Egyptians] came
to dread the Israelites. The Egyptians ruthlessly imposed upon
the Israelites the various labors that they made them perform.
Ruthlessly they made life bitter for them with harsh labor
at mortar and bricks and with all sorts of tasks in the field.
(Exod 1:8–14)

What does it mean for a people to transition from workers to slaves? What shifted in the lives of the Israelites as their
autonomy was slowly stripped away, one decree at a time? They
were still fed, presumably; the biblical story makes no reference to widespread hunger. Perhaps their compensation was
reduced; maybe they failed to receive wage increases they had
rightfully earned. But the text suggests something else.

Their managers "started to look at the Israelites with disgust
and dread" (Exod 1:12 CEB). They made the Israelites' lives
miserable with hard labor and cruel work. Oppression was not
simply more work; it was a different quality of work. This work
denied their dignity. In the eyes of their Egyptian taskmasters,
the Israelites ceased to be human. They devolved into a set of
instruments, mere tools for accomplishing the empire's project.
And it was no small project.

Pyramid construction required a massive, organized workforce. Erecting monuments with enduring stability demanded
painstaking engineering—expertise from above—and careful
control of the workers who carried it out below. Neither loyalty
nor a commonly internalized purpose could be assumed. The
more feared scenario was that the slaves would "join our enemies in fighting against us and rise from the ground" (Exod
1:10). Maybe worse, they could unionize.

The pyramids not only cut outlines into the Gizan desert horizon; they were imprinted on Moses's innermost instincts too. The early Exodus stories suggest in Moses an internal tension; even as he adopts the entitled affect of a prince, he leans toward identification with the community of Israelite slaves he was born into. The line between slave and ruler is clear, and Moses finds belonging on neither side of it. And so, he retreats. He escapes to Midian, busies himself in an invisible position, shepherding his father-in-law's sheep—away from the pyramids but still very much in their shadow.

A long time passes. The Exodus narrative continues:

> A long time after that, the king of Egypt died. The Israelites were groaning under the bondage and cried out; and their cry for help from the bondage rose up to God. God heard their moaning, and God remembered the covenant with Abraham and Isaac and Jacob. God looked upon the Israelites, and God took notice of them. (Exod 2:23–25).

And one day, far enough from home to be susceptible to visions, Moses sees an unnatural glinting in the sun. It's a scrubby desert plant that appears to hold flame without being destroyed by it. The air around the blaze is charged with sound, a voice that carries the bass sound of authority and yet takes in the smallness of this man who has tried to disappear. The voice is intentional, focused; it names Moses as it identifies itself. "I am the God of your father's [house]—the God of Abraham, the God of Isaac, and the God of Jacob" (Exod 3:6). Moses hides his face, fearful at having been noticed, named by this voice. The voice of God continues:

> I have marked well the plight of My people in Egypt and have heeded their outcry because of their taskmasters; yes, I am mindful of their sufferings.
>   I have come down to rescue them from the Egyptians and to bring them out of that land to a good and spacious land, a land

*flowing with milk and honey, the region of the Canaanites, the
Hittites, the Amorites, the Perizzites, the Hivites, and the Jeb-
usites. Now the cry of the Israelites has reached Me; moreover,
I have seen how the Egyptians oppress them. Come, therefore,
I will send you to Pharaoh, and you shall free My people, the
Israelites, from Egypt. (Exod 3:7–10)*

The empathetic instinct in this story is God's, not Moses's.
Moses responds reluctantly, still trying to retreat. At this point,
Moses is neither visionary nor self-motivated. He is hesitant
not only about his qualifications for leadership but about every
aspect of the liberation project. No part of him is animated by
the challenge God sets before him, either as a matter of faith
or of meager self-confidence. No matter what assistance God
offers, Moses poses another question, a further objection. He is
like the proverbial naysayer in every organization's budgeting
committee, convinced that their value lies in identifying and
embracing every reason to say no.

No, Moses is not yet a leader. He was not born a leader, nor
is he transformed into one by dint of God's anointing. He cannot see past the image that he carries with him from life in
the empire. There, the only leaders are ones who look like Pharaoh. They sit alone, capably, imperially, far above the people
they direct. They cast vision with conviction. They lead fear-
lessly, their followers faithful in their efforts. This is the image
of leadership that Moses holds inside him as he reluctantly
turns toward God's call. He has a long way to go before he will
become a leader like no other.

Notes

1 This is a cumulative song with thirteen verses, usually sung joyfully
at the end of the Passover Seder. It is a favorite among children,
designed to add fun and lightheartedness to the experience.
2 Based on the Greek *epikomon* (dessert), the *afikomen* is a half-piece
of *matzah* that adults hide early in the Seder. After dinner, the

children are invited to search for it, and the finder is usually treated with some sort of prize as a reward. The *afikomen* is then split among participants as a final dessert to conclude the meal.

3   The Four Questions are traditionally recited by the youngest person at the table, and the preparation is so anxiety-provoking that you can ask just about any fifty-year-old Jewish person who hasn't been to synagogue in three decades and they'll be able to chant the Four Questions, verbatim and pitch-perfect.

4   The Seder is a ritual meal that celebrates the ancient Israelites' liberation from slavery in Egypt. It centers on intergenerational storytelling and foods that evoke memories of being strangers in a strange land.

5   The triangle image is everywhere present in the Christian tradition. It is a central image in Christianity's concept of the divine Trinity. We hope to distinguish here a triangle from a pyramid; a triangle turns and can be an equality-promoting image. See Richard Rohr and Mike Morrell, *The Divine Dance* (New Kensington, PA: Whitaker House, 2016).

6   Christina Baldwin and Ann Linnea, *The Circle Way* (Oakland, CA: Berrett-Koehler, 2010), 10.

7   Walter Brueggemann, *The Prophetic Imagination* (Philadelphia: Fortress, 1978), 26–30.

8   Brueggemann, *Prophetic Imagination*, 35.

9   Jeremy Heimans and Henry Tims, *New Power: How Power Works in Our Hyperconnected World—and How to Make It Work for You* (New York: Anchor, 2018), 1.

10   Andy Crouch, *Playing God: Redeeming the Gift of Power* (Downers Grove, IL: InterVarsity, 2013), 16.

CHAPTER TWO

Cracks in the Façade

There are time-tested reasons why we prefer putting people into pyramids when we're organizing for action. First and foremost, they help us get things done. Clarity of roles smooths the way for ambition to manifest into achievement and eases the anxiety of everyone involved. One of the earliest stories in the biblical tradition mythologizes the power of collective endeavor.

> *Everyone on earth had the same language and the same words. And as they migrated from the east, they came upon a valley in the land of Shinar and settled there.*
> *They said to one another, "Come, let us make bricks and burn them hard."—Brick served them as stone, and bitumen served them as mortar.—And they said, "Come, let us build us a city, and a tower with its top in the sky, to make a name for ourselves; else we shall be scattered all over the world."* (Gen 11:1–4)

The collective "let us" in that passage is actually a singular voice. One leader, one city, one tower. The kind of building project that could only be accomplished among people of one mind and intention. Almost certainly, dissenters and skeptics were consigned to unthinking labor, implementing the architectural vision of a leader whose goal was to "make a name for ourselves."

But there is no ambiguity in the conclusion of this biblical story. A single tower reaching up to heaven was decidedly not God's vision for the still-new creation. God cleverly calls a stop to the building project—not by knocking it down but by multiplying the languages spoken by the people. The workers simply cannot understand the commands of their managers. They are confused, they disperse; the tower, along with the community that built it, is abandoned.

In the biblical narrative, the architecture among the people of God after this incident returned to low-rise, and it remained so for a long time. For generations, the tribes of ancient Israel lived close to the earth, housing themselves on flat ground. Towering structures do not appear again in the Bible's chronology until generations later, when the descendants of Abraham are enslaved in Egypt.

Towers, pyramids, temples, cathedrals—massive, labor-intensive structures—these are the ornaments of human achievement. The wonders of the ancient world feature tall buildings, symbols of accomplishment great civilizations have left behind. Their construction repeatedly calls societies to concerted action. But they also embody, in their demand for nameless, faceless labor, the instruments of oppression. The ending to the Tower of Babel story represents a sharp disruption to human progress. But the story suggests disruption was precisely the divine point. Perhaps, we are meant to hear, we distort the intentionally wild beauty of creation whenever we instrumentalize people, every time we regard them as merely useful equipment for our ambitions and plans, no matter how important or impressive.

And yet, it is order that enables cooperative human endeavor. Our preference for it is not inherently faithless. Creation itself began with God's Spirit hovering over formless water, as if there were no place to land until the roiling (*tohu va'vohu*, Gen 1:2) could be stilled. Chaos and anarchy may be fascinating, but—in the biblical tradition, at least—they do not point toward progress.

Perhaps it was God's initiative toward ordering the universe that inspired the human drive for orderliness. As it did for creation, order gives us a stable starting point from which to begin our work. Its patterns salve our discomfort; its consistency calms our anxiety. We prefer it to the messy, slow processes of witness, of encounter, of negotiating our differences. We choose order almost always, even when it conflicts with the values of our faith.

Pyramid-shaped organizations, their power exercised from the top, are quite adept at getting things done. Leadership that pauses for peripheral hearing is surely less predictable. Its outcomes are less certain. The sound of one voice sounds like clarity; too many threatens cacophony. So when human beings are stressed, when deadlines grow near, when our patience runs thin, we revert to order and predictability. We snap back into certainty, like rubber bands released from tension. The familiarity of hierarchy, the tidiness of established seats of power, the comforting reliance on the voice of a strong, singular leader—this is our organizational base camp.

The Leadership of "Great Men"

Because the pyramid is so deeply embedded in Western culture, it should not come as a surprise that much of our leadership language mirrors its shape.[1] Leaders rise to the top. Only a few are ordained—called out—from all the rest. Everyone else is consigned to a designated slot in a cascading configuration of positions—fewer close to the top, many more in supportive roles near the base.

The earliest and most persistent theories of organizational leadership focus on the unique personal qualities of notable leaders: charisma, vision, courage, even exceptional faithfulness—all summarized into the historical great-man theory.[2] Today that theory sounds wrong to us in a thousand ways. It reeks of gender, racial, and cultural supremacy. But the concept's endurance reveals an abiding, accepted truth about leadership: like mythological heroes, the most effective leaders set themselves apart from everyone else.

Organizations that are led by these kinds of mythological leaders have, historically, had the greatest chances of producing what history looks back on as great success. The strongest nations have the most skillful heads of state. The most profitable companies are led by the most capable CEOs. The best churches have the most gifted pastors, who regularly inspire others to follow their vision. These leaders bring people along. They know how to smooth out the rough edges of conflicting opinions; they make sure everyone is on board, working from the same script. The most self-assured leaders may countenance opposition, but they are unswayed by it; they find a way to assuage contradictions, to dismiss dissent.

Not surprisingly, the Egyptian pharaohs, revered as gods in their own right, favored this heliocentric model of leadership. Every decree, demand, and directive required access to the sun, so pharaohs positioned themselves, both figuratively and literally, directly above all others. This configuration was quite effective for building unparalleled achievements, but the danger of a system that clusters around the sun is that everybody gets burned. In congregational terms, this constellation, which we sometimes think of as a cult of personality, often means that congregants and laypeople grow weary, disillusioned, and disengaged. Assembling around one leader's magnetism warms everyone for a while, but it almost inevitably leads to disempowerment of staff members and volunteers, which then matures into boredom. And the senior leader—the sun at the center of it all—burns out in short order, leaving the whole organization out in the cold.

Gatekeepers and Truth Tellers

Today, people are leaving the organized religious complex in droves. The reasons for their emigration are many, but surely among them is a disconnect between the institution's insatiable hunger for a reliable base of rock-solid support and the ready availability of other resources for spiritual flourishing that anyone can pick up, often without significant cost or commitment. The rushing current away from houses of worship and other religious institutions is a cry for our attention. There is simply too wide a gap between the constraining institutions we've built and the expansive freedom people seek—and that the biblical narrative promises. The reparative work before us is perhaps less about preserving (or regaining) institutional vigor and more about listening to members who did not return to church after pandemic isolation, to the majority of young people who have not followed the churchgoing traditions of their parents and grandparents, to the many who gather inspiration from online platforms rather than pews, and to the growing multitude of clergy who are leaving their positions in ministry altogether.

Perhaps these are the truth tellers. They have watched the gatekeepers of organized religion hoard power, money, and privilege so that the institution can feed itself. They are tired of the pleas for institutional loyalty, the endless cycles of unrecognized effort at the bottom. They are disillusioned and disheartened by the ways religion's structure constricts the spaciousness of the world they seek for themselves and for others.

This trend of disaffiliation that is so evident in religious institutions is not unique. It's in our institutions of higher education, in our political organizations, and in the workforce, too. The so-called Great Resignation of the early 2020s is the echo of a similar expression in the workplace. The disengaged point accusingly at false and misleading narratives as they walk out the door. "We will not be entombed in your cubicles," they are saying. "We don't trust the constraining dimensions of your institutions to hold our aspirations for our lives."

From Formative to Performative

In his book *A Time to Build*, Yuval Levin explores this trend of institutional drift and identifies an alarming pattern: the institutions that were once trusted to form our character and our culture have devolved into centers of performative politics, performative education, and performative faith.

> This transformation . . . of the character of our institutions has not come out of nowhere. It has been driven by the same forces that have underlain the broader evolution of our society over the past half century. . . . Over the decades, our popular culture has increasingly become a celebrity culture, in which exposure, prominence, audience, and the appearance of authenticity are paramount. In many domains of American life, this has tended to blur the distinction between reality and image, and this logic could hardly have avoided penetrating our core institutions.[3]

This trend, which elevates a few and relegates everyone else to passiveness, is evident in politics, where our congressional leaders seem to care more about their Twitter following than about passing meaningful legislation. It's true in education, where teaching to the test has had widespread effects on the overall quality of education, especially in minoritized communities. It's true in finance, where the democratizing potential of blockchain technology shaped the mythology of cryptocurrency and subsequently skyrocketed the value of a myriad of coins, despite the lack of any demonstrable utility as anything beyond gambling chips. It should come as no surprise to us that each of these three domains has slid down the Gallup Institutional Confidence Index in recent decades.[4] The more performative each domain becomes, the less credibility it carries. And—to our dismay—the same holds true with respect to organized religion.

From Eternity to Entertainment

As twentieth-century cultural forces questioned and then steered away from inherited traditions, many religious institutions followed their lead. Relevance seemed to demand some sweetening of our ancient rites, some adjustment of our defining missional course. The evidence for modernization was visible: megachurches grew and flourished by modeling themselves less after the modest faith communities of our ancestors and more after a high-production blend of capitalism and celebrity. Attendance metrics ticked up in response to higher production values in worship services. Charisma begat growth. Growth begat celebrity. Faith leaders scrambled to create a personal brand, trying to keep up with the Osteens.

By the late 1980s, celebrity pastors could readily be found on television screens every Sunday morning. Suddenly, the modest aspirations of the folks who first laid brick on brick in local communities seemed inadequate to meet the appetites whetted by popular culture. Every traditional faith organization had to think about becoming and remaining culturally relevant; and often, mission took a back seat to modernity. Founding ideals gave way to catchy slogans. Anxiety about survival fueled a whole movement focused on church growth and not much more. We still speak of our concern with shaping identities and building character, but our actions point to a different set of goals. They drive us toward the tireless (and increasingly fruitless) pursuit of the three B's—butts, budgets, and buildings.[5]

Whom Do We Serve?

In the economy that has most emphatically shaped us, profit supersedes purpose. But unlike commercial enterprises, religious organizations are not in the business of either producing a device or delivering a service to be marketed. Measurements of effectiveness are elusive; it's not easy to quantify the results of efforts to build new habits of the heart. The Christian imperative of the Great Commission sends us out to give away the life and teachings of Jesus without thought of return. Countless texts in Jewish tradition call on us to leave the world better than it was when we got here. These calls demand that we honor human dignity above all else. In a faith-based ethic, the reach of our good works is intended to be broad, free, undiscriminating, in the image of a Creator who makes the sun rise on both the evil and the good and sends rain to bless both the righteous and the unrighteous (Matt 5:45). There are no earthly profits to be gained, no privilege of ownership or commercial success that attaches to the transmission of divine attention, compassion, and creativity.

And we try to follow this model, we really do. Across a broad spectrum of theologies, people of faith share a common purpose of making a way for the love of God to inspire our communities and the world. Most congregations engage in faithful work that aims to bless the lives of persons who are not (yet) members. But the practical reality of everyday congregational leadership focuses elsewhere. Whatever the stated public mission of the organization is, and no matter how genuinely it is subscribed to, it is also driven by a private mission, as the church consultant Gil Rendle writes in *Countercultural: Subversive Resistance and the Neighborhood Congregation.*[6] The truth in most congregations is that its workforce—the people engaged in the generous, benevolent work of the congregation—are also its primary customers. The hungriest consumers of churches' and leaders' resources are the organization's inner constituencies. As much as pastors might wish that time could be wrested away for more outwardly focused action, it's our members, volunteers, and donors who (rightfully) expect our most faithful attention.

Do we serve our congregants or employ them? Clergy leaders can be forgiven for their confusion; the messages are mixed, the metaphors contradictory. We are servants who replicate the self-sacrifice of Christ. We are spiritual and moral exemplars. We are "great men" who influence others by the power of our vision and charisma. We are all of these things and none of these things all at once.

The business consultant Warren Bennis, in his foreword to the scholar Sharon Daloz Parks's important book *Leadership Can Be Taught*, begins: "The illusion is obstinate and enduring: A mortal is seemingly anointed by the gods, typically at the moment of conception, and is stamped with a unique gift that allows him or her to lead others. This person shines irrepressibly, and other mere mortals are compelled to follow."[7]

This was our formative vision. Many of us who entered religious leadership hoped that our sense of calling meant attending to our spiritual lives, modeling our attentiveness after the biblical shepherds (who no doubt loved the sheep assigned them), and relying on our God-given people skills to equip us fully for congregational leadership. We know now: it is not enough.

The Value of Ordinary Faith

In coming-of-age ceremonies (bar, bat, b-mitzvahs) in synagogues, frequently the first person to speak to the teenager after they chant from the Torah says, "Good job!"—as if the only purpose of attaining adult status in the Jewish community is to successfully perform in front of a crowd. The message that performance is the goal has seeped not only into leaders; we've woven it into the ritual fabric of our communities, too. The more emphasis we put on performance, the less valuable ordinary faith becomes.

For congregational leaders, the effect of this performance imperative is subtle but insidious. We wonder whether our congregation's sluggishness is evidence of its leader's mere mortality, the shortage of our personal talent to adequately inspire. The improvements we've tried to make to the organizations we lead seem, on reflection, elusive and short-lived. Perhaps vibrant congregational life exists more in our imaginations than in reality, we worry. Maybe humble leadership is a thing of the past. Or maybe it still lives on—but where? Whatever success is, it is out of our reach.

Leaders look to the charismatic few who direct mega-churches and synagogues with national audiences, and we know we are not them. To be sure, we have mixed feelings about these celebrity leaders. It can seem presumptuous, ego-driven, even distasteful, to emulate the self-conscious style of these chosen ones. The model seems antithetical to the values that describe a spiritual life: generosity, humility, transparency. We have seen, all too often, the disasters that ego-driven, messianic church leaders cause, the damage they do to the churches and people they lead. But still, their leadership successes are almost universally envied.

Doing Damage

For the past five decades, Gallup has asked Americans about the degree to which they trust a variety of important American institutions: banks, Congress, public schools, the Supreme Court, and a number of others. For fifty years running, Americans' confidence in religious organizations has declined precipitously. So much so, in fact, that even in our hyperpolarized political culture, Americans trust the presidency (38 percent) more than organized religion (37 percent).[8] In a cultural moment in which half of all Americans are convinced that we will have a politically incited civil war in the next few years, organized religion is even less trustworthy than the political vehicles driving us there.[9]

There are more and less obvious reasons for this steep decline in trust. Understanding how we lost it is a critical step toward making the kind of changes that might restore people's confidence. Let's start with the low-hanging fruit.

Absolute Power Corrupts Absolutely

The Catholic Church

One need look no further than the sprawling, explosive revelations from the Catholic Church abuse scandals to understand why faith in faith has eroded.[10] Not only did those entrusted with the care of children abuse them, but those priests at the center of the scandal were defended by the full institutional power of the church. When the heat of suspicion or allegations grew too intense, the system closed around the wrongdoers; often, they were merely relocated to a new community, where they would prey on innocent children and repeat the cycle all over again.

Pope Francis has called for the church to right itself, arguing for a reorganized power structure in the Catholic Church, an "inverted pyramid" that would put trust and power back in the hands of parishioners.[11] It's a bold image whose realization is a long way away.

The Southern Baptist Convention

When you first open the full Guidepost Solutions investigative report detailing abuse in the Southern Baptist Convention, it's the sheer volume that is immediately shocking. The report, which followed a sprawling seven-month investigation into allegations of sexual abuse by clergy and cover-up by denominational leaders, is 288 pages. The stories are laid out on page after page, in case after case, of pastors and others in power harassing congregants, assaulting community members, and breaking a staggering variety of laws along the way.

The report also details the tireless efforts of the convention to keep these stories in the dark. They intimidated, stonewalled, and publicly denigrated victims for years.[12] In a significant number of cases, they kept many of the 703 accused perpetrators in their positions long after damning accusations had come to light. Perpetrators were walled off and defended even when their conduct was declared criminal. Denominational machinery propped up the power of abusers, sometimes with the consent of their congregations. Victims remained in their pews Sunday after Sunday while those who had preyed on them preached a gospel of righteousness and love. The institutional decay reflected in this report is profoundly troubling.

Hebrew Union College
Just one month before the report that rocked the Southern Baptist Convention was released, another similar, though smaller-scale, investigative report was released. It focused on Hebrew Union College-Jewish Institute of Religion, the Jewish seminary founded in 1875. North America's first Jewish institution of higher education, Hebrew Union College has been a cornerstone of American Jewish life for almost 150 years. Through its affiliation with the progressive Reform Movement, Hebrew Union College has often led the movement toward serious shifts in Jewish cultural life. From the ordination of women, to the full participation of LGBTQ+ leaders, to its early integration of social justice efforts, Hebrew Union College has exemplified the growing, socially conscious edge of Jewish life in the United States and worldwide for decades.

The report, which (to Hebrew Union College's credit) they hosted on their own website in order to step into accountability, revealed widespread and long-existing abuse at the seminary. For five decades, Hebrew Union College faculty had been the subjects of a dizzying array of valid accusations, including sexual harassment, gender discrimination, discrimination against LGBTQ+ individuals, bullying, and racial discrimination. But even repeated abuse in religious organizations is not always newsworthy these days. The investigators reported a clear pattern of "abuse of power by some administrative leaders and faculty, and fear of retaliation by the reporters or would-be reporters of that abuse."[13] News that the institution had ignored victims' testimony for decades while it buttressed support for the accused faculty members was both startling and startlingly commonplace.

Corrosive Power

What explains this alarming pattern of power and abuse in institutions that started with benevolent intentions? When he compared the brains of powerful leaders and not-so-powerful people, the neuroscientist Subkhvinder Obhi found neurological evidence that over time, people in powerful positions can gradually lose their empathy—their ability to detect what others are feeling or to see themselves as others see them.[14] They laugh less with others; they are less adept at picking up on social cues. The psychology researcher Dacher Keltner calls this the power paradox.[15] Over time, people in positions of power lose the very capacity to connect that originally brought them currency in their relationships with others. With decreasing ability to empathize and to mirror the experiences of others, these leaders become emotionally and professionally isolated.[16] They lose the ability to identify in themselves and in others "the sound of the genuine" that Howard Thurman spoke of.[17] They navigate the world guided only by their personal vision, rather than any shared perspective.[18] And sometimes, the institutions that have put these leaders in power continue to be ruled by them long after the cracks in their humanity have become visible.

Faith and Fanaticism

Gallup's Institutional Confidence Index has tracked a steady decline in religion for over five decades and running. But the descent is not exactly even. A closer look, examining year by year rather than decade by decade, reveals one year when the slow drip looks more like a breaking levee. Between 2001 and

2002, Americans' confidence in religious institutions dropped from 60 percent to 45 percent—the largest one-year drop for religion and among the largest one-year dips of any institution in the fifty-year history of the survey.

On September 11, 2001, nineteen al-Qaeda hijackers orchestrated and implemented the most deadly attack on American soil in US history. There have been countless investigations, reports, books, and theories that seek to explain why. Understanding the motivations for the attack felt critically important for Americans trying to make sense of one of the most senseless acts in American history, and suggestions ranged from geopolitical tensions, to a desire to undermine US efforts abroad, to revenge. But in the end, whether we were reading Osama Bin Laden's November 2002 "Letter to America," or the results of one of countless investigative reports, or just the newspaper, one theme emerged: this was not just an act of political terrorism. This was an act of religious extremism.

Christian and Jewish houses of worship saw a brief uptick in participation immediately after 9/11, but the longer-term impact was different. For many Americans, the attack shook the foundations of goodwill toward all religious practice. Muslims became the focus of rising hatred and attacks and continue to be singled out over two decades later. But it turns out that *all* religions suffered on the heels of 9/11. Once the synaptic connection between faith and fanaticism was made, Americans immediately grew wary of religious certitude, unchecked authority figures, and religion writ large.

The September 11 attack, just one incident in a sharp rise in religious violence around the world,[19] demonstrated visibly just how dangerous religious fervor can be. The danger soars in non-Western cultures where autocratic leaders hold unchecked authority and those at the bottom are expected to obey without question. But even in the United States, where the pyramids tend to have a gentler slope, the damage to Americans' confidence in religion was severe. After the instinctive and brief turn toward institutions that offered Americans comfort and respite, the attack eventually gave new fuel to the movement toward disaffiliation from religious adherence of every kind.

Widening Cracks

The reasons for religious institutions' decline have been exhaustively described and analyzed. Religion has failed one of its central roles: to renew people's confidence in a narrative that promises, "All shall be well." We live in a moment of cascading crises, not only in American religion but in America writ large. We are more polarized, more isolated, angrier, and more pained than ever before. Innovators and entrepreneurs may lead the way, but it is communities of faith and their commitment to the common good that democratize the potential for transformation. The compassion and generosity seeded by the stories that inspire faith might still reweave the torn fabric of our society. But the structures that hold these stories, the institutions charged with preserving and transmitting them, have cracked under excessive weight from the top, from disintegration at the bottom, and by the occasion of earthquakes they were not built to withstand. Our religious communities are working hard to make it through the narrows of this tumultuous moment. But if we are to emerge on the other side strengthened and ready to form a new generation in hope and love, the cracks must be repaired, not just taped over. Change must be substantive, and it must start at the top.

Inside, Something Is Stirring: Eugene Kim's Story

From the moment people meet Eugene Kim—whether in person, on Zoom, or just by reading his latest tweets[20]—many are certain that he was destined to be a leader. He connects with people eye to eye and listens with remarkable intent, mirroring back what he hears but with even greater clarity and eloquence. He has that rare capacity to preach in a way that makes people feel like they were supposed to be there on that very day, to hear that very word. His Twitter timeline manages to convey fearless, prophetic critique of corruption and injustice along with an inspiring vision of a world healed—a world that he insists is still within our grasp.

But unlike many of his peers, Kim was not called into faith leadership from a young age. Or, if he was being called, he was quite determined not to answer. Despite a lifelong yearning to live a life of purpose, to do "something real" in this world,[21] he felt sure that he wouldn't be able to do either of those in the church.

> I grew up in Korean immigrant churches, which tend to be fairly hierarchical. It's a cultural thing. Everything is structured around age, title, gender. There's a pecking order in terms of power. But it's a high power-distance culture, and so that translates to a very high power-distance spirituality. And I think probably early on, I didn't have the language for it, but that's probably what I bristled against the most in my spiritual journey. It was the disconnect between those who were the empowered voices in the system and (the rest of us). And so I went through distancing myself from that whole world.[22]

Kim couldn't see himself in the traditional mold of a faith leader: the sage on the stage who shifts into preacher-speak during sermons,[23] who keeps distance from the community, who serves more as a spiritual exemplar than a companion and counselor. But as his teen years yielded to adulthood and he sifted through the inner stirrings that had pushed him to find a significant purpose for himself, he called into question the beliefs that had been instilled in him about how a faith leader should look, sound, and act. Perhaps, he thought, ministry was not the one-size-fits-all robe of his childhood impressions. Maybe he could bring his own imagination to the role. Maybe he could be a radically different kind of faith leader than he had seen growing up.

Finding a Voice

Early in his career, Kim came upon an enticing opportunity: to serve as the second pastor of a rapidly growing Asian church in the Boston area, where the possibilities for expansion—of the church and of his own leadership skills—seemed limitless. Years later, he realized that there was also at work in him another, less conscious draw to this role. The lead pastor, a highly talented and charismatic preacher who had founded and built this predominantly Asian church, was white. The child of immigrants, Kim had been taught from childhood to do well in school, work hard, and earn his keep as a means to fit in. The way you do that, he had internalized, is "you become adjacent to whiteness."[24] So when the opportunity to stand next to this leader presented itself, Kim saw—although he was not fully aware of it at the time—a fitting fulfillment of those formative childhood lessons.

At the church, the other Asian congregants were also eager not only to be adjacent to white culture but to yield to it. Kim says, "They made a conscious decision not to serve Asian food, not to wear black,[25] never to speak the language. I think we weren't aware of how we were accommodating to dominant culture by erasing and silencing our own minority culture."[26]

The dynamics were complex from the beginning. Even so, Kim's early years in his role as second-seat pastor were remarkably fruitful—for him, for his growing family, and for the entire community.

Complementary Gifts

For several years, Kim's position at the church allowed him to advance the values that had first drawn him into ministry: generosity, collaboration, curiosity. He stayed intently focused on lifting up those around him. For every word of praise he received about his leadership, Kim responded by redirecting it to the church's lay leaders. Each new stage of growth for the organization was, he reminded congregants, a reflection of its members more than its pastors. In Eugene's vision, the members did not belong to the church; the church belonged to them.

Even serving as the number two in their leadership team, Kim was remarkably effective; their small start-up church became a sprawling, established organization with multiple campuses and a dizzying array of ministries that served an increasingly diverse community. In the early years, the two pastors designed portfolios that built on each of their respective skill sets. Their working spheres were complementary. Especially because the demands of the growing community outweighed its staffing structure, they were careful to avoid overlap and redundancies in their responsibilities. With growth as their goal, efficiency was crowned king. For a while, at least, their dual leadership arrangement worked just fine, Kim says. "That worked for many, many years, predominantly because we were such different people that our gifts were quite complementary. He did his thing and I did mine. There wasn't a whole lot of overlap. And that's actually what made us a very good team over the years. He covered my blind spots, I covered his. That's what enabled us to create an effective organization."[27]

Renegotiating Roles

As the church shape-shifted over the years, the two pastors checked in regularly. Communication helped ensure that each of them stayed inside their respective arenas of responsibility. From time to time, they needed a conversation that probed deeper than a simple check-in. "Every few years, we would pause and negotiate. 'OK, what's your job? What's my job? Where do I end? Where do you begin? And where are the overlaps?'"[28]

Like most pastors, these two were practiced at answering the question, What do you do? The answers were myriad: We make sure that the trains run on time, that the work gets done, the rites are given, the sermons written, the services delivered. The urgencies have to be prioritized, the emails answered, the fires put out. We rise to every occasion because that's what we do. Because that's what we're called to do. For both of them, it was more than just a job; it was a sacred pursuit.

As his work progressed, though, Kim began to notice a gap between the growing list of what he was doing and what he actually felt called to do. Like most leaders, he had to make himself stop before saying yes. Like many pastors, he had a big stack of books waiting to be read. It was too easy to get by without taking sabbatical time or even a faithfully taken day off each week. There were countless reasons to defer investing time and energy into anything other than the church.

Occasionally, Kim would ask himself: Who am I becoming? Even productive discussions around titles and responsibilities could not answer those questions. As intentional as these two pastors had been about separating their roles, Kim could feel himself running out of room to grow. The church, and his position inside its pyramid, was stifling his process of becoming.

> It started to come to a point when our gifts were less complementary. He had the stronger voice, but I was finding my own voice as well. And so we kept trying to renegotiate our working relationship. It got to a point where I think we were just like, "OK, we're not necessarily seeing things the same exact way, and we're both occupying very important positions in the system, in the structure." The last modification we made was I was supposed to be the lead pastor of our main campus. He was supposed to level up and operate at more of a multi-campus role. But . . . the founder's trap became apparent. He never actually left the main campus. And at a certain point, he suggested that it might be time for me to go.[29]

Kim tried to salvage the two pastors' relationship and his position in the community he had poured almost half of his life into building. He suggested they talk openly and vulnerably about their situation. He named the power dynamics in the leadership they were supposed to share, including those around race. Perhaps, he suggested, there was a co-leadership model that would better reflect their history: for almost two decades they had built this church together. Kim still wanted to believe that their complementary skills and passions would allow them to flourish again if they could find more equity in their partnership.

But Kim was bone-weary; probably they both were. He was aware of the statistics about the staggering levels of burnout in ministry. Some twelve hundred clergy were quitting the pulpit every month in America,[30] and that number was on the rise. Why succumb to their profession's inevitable exhaustion when they could live into a different kind of leadership, guided by collaboration, equity, and generosity? Why not experiment with a co-leadership model that would create more than enough space for both of them to grow? Wouldn't that kind of model yield exponential returns for the community's growth, too?

But change would not be easy.

> Our structure as an organization, our system, was simply not designed for co-leadership or a true equitable partnership. It was really designed to have just one leader. So as long as I agreed to follow the leader, I could stay. But after seventeen years of being the second leader (or maybe it was first follower?), I felt I needed the room to grow and use my own voice, too, not just make my boss's voice better. Ultimately, I faced the hard reality that if I wanted to live fully into who I was becoming, I would have to leave. I simply ran out of room. And so that's when I left. I didn't have anything. I had no idea what I was going to do.[31]

Who Wins?

For seventeen years, Kim and his colleague worked together productively. They used their respective gifts and passions to transform a small community into a dynamic, bustling, multicampus church, the kind of congregation most pastors only dream about. Each of them grew in their personal leadership capability. They'd wrestled with complicated power dynamics; the race issues alone would have been enough to undermine most working relationships. They'd navigated difficult terrain together, recalibrated their compass as needed. They'd stayed in leadership together for a long time. The dissolution of their partnership is not a story about heroes and villains, or one about winners and losers. It's far too complex to be broken down into binaries.

Perhaps the most culpable party was lurking behind them all along, an ominous and invisible backdrop to their tireless efforts from day one. Empire—which shows up in this story cloaked in a variety of garbs: whiteness, hierarchy, othering— fought back progress, every step of the way. It thwarted the spirit of even their most intentional collaboration. The fierce compulsion toward church growth, to keep engaging new people and those whose engagement was slipping, heaped more and more jobs onto the pastors' plates; they could see it in every one of their check-ins over the years. The drive for success is unrelenting, compassionless. Empire is hard-hearted toward everyone, even those who find their place atop the pyramid.

The Limits of Heroism

The hero's journey, described by the writer Joseph Campbell, captures and articulates the empire's mythology of individual greatness.[32] A hero is shaped by a journey that invokes risk and endures hardship. The endeavor requires persistence, inexhaustible personal passion. Along the way, the protagonist is transformed into a hero. The formation that happens is individual, not collective. It might take a village to equip the leader, and a team of faithful soldiers to battle alongside is helpful, but once the ordeal is over, it is a single hero who is revealed and who reaps the reward. And as Christina Baldwin and Ann Linnea note in *The Circle Way*, once heroes indulge in their rewards, they are exceedingly unlikely to share them. This is our heroic story, they say: the rise to power and the escape to greater freedom.[33]

The irony of the hero's story, of course, is that the powerful seat atop a pyramid offers even less freedom than anywhere else in the structure. The primary work of many leaders becomes keeping that job, maintaining the status quo, sustaining the system as it is. For Eugene Kim, the system wasn't worth sustaining, let alone sacrificing any more of his gifts for. When the realization came that there was room for only one at the peak of his church, the only way for him to move forward was to break free from the pyramid completely: "Ultimately, I faced the hard reality that if I wanted to live fully into who I was becoming, I would have to leave. I simply ran out of room. And though I tried, there was no option provided for me to stay AND be true to my own process. So it became clear that it was time for me to go."[34]

It was freedom that Kim sought as he stepped outside the pyramid that had held his career, his life, and his faith. If there was no room for his gifts and his calling at the top of the institution he knew, he would have to take the risk of finding his place in a less towering structure.

Small Openings:
Moses's Story

Moses has heard God speak. The sight of the burning bush stays with him. Emboldened by his calling, God's confidence in him, Moses makes his first leader-like move. He goes directly to Pharaoh. He shares his newly minted credentials and proposes a tactical first step. "Let my people go out into the desert for a festival to the Lord," he suggests. "Just three days" (Exod 5:1, 3). He waits for a response. Surely Pharaoh will see that the little Hebrew boy who grew up as an adopted grandson in the Egyptian court is now a colleague, a man worthy of respect, and that Moses bears his own measure of divine authority. Moses is no longer a supplicant; he has been elevated to the top of his own, if smaller, pyramid. His eyes now meet Pharaoh's straight across.

Only Pharaoh is unimpressed. He rejects Moses's overture with a demonstration of his obviously greater power. He issues an edict: effective immediately, the Israelite slaves will add to their duties the collection of straw that is necessary to the composition of bricks. There will be no concession in their daily quotas. The only consequence of Moses's empowerment is the people's greater oppression.

What happened? Moses returns to God. "Surely this is not my fault. You have done nothing to rescue your people!" he complains. "You gave me power, but it's not working" (Exod 5:22–23, paraphrased).

Again God affirms a commitment to the Hebrew slaves. They are still the heirs of God's promises. Again God takes note of the people's now even greater desperation. What Moses has met is an obstacle, not the end of the road. "I have not forgotten," God speaks.

This is what Moses needed to hear. His hope is rekindled. He turns to the beleaguered slave people, offers the promises God has made and now repeated to him—to save the people from their bondage, to transport and deliver them to a wholly different place, to make of them a people distinguished from all the rest. The text is spare, but we can imagine the expectations Moses carries with him from this moment. He has regathered his confidence. He speaks with the authority he believes he has been given. He is the carrier of great gifts. The very deity of the

Israelites' ancestors has spoken. God's attention has been captured irrevocably. Relief is at hand.

Except that, when Moses delivers God's powerful promises, the people do not seem comforted. The announcement that what looks like Pharaoh's defiance is only an insignificant, temporary setback is met with a resounding blankness. Skeptical, disheartened faces stare back at Moses. His motivational speech is swallowed into the ground. The writer of Exodus explains, "They didn't listen to Moses because of their complete exhaustion and their hard labor" (Exod 6:9).

These people have lived inside the confines of the pyramid for too long to be able to imagine what awaits them outside its walls. They are exhausted, depleted of imagination, drained of hope. Their trust is not as buoyant as Moses's. He may have heard the God of their ancestors speak, but they have not. Despite his exuberance, his hope is anything but contagious.

Pastoral leaders tell a story of salvation, what we imagine God wants for our people, for all of creation. We proclaim good news: freedom from the false structures that bind us, divine connection, the fullness of our humanity. We tell it from the front, or the top, or wherever the pulpit stands in our tradition. We expect our listeners to hear and to be moved. We hope they will be inspired, reassured by our words. But even our most fervent preaching or visionary prophecy does not always implant confidence or faith. Messages of human wholeness must be experienced firsthand; they are often lost in translation, no matter how eloquent the messenger.

Perhaps this is Moses's—and every leader's—most essential work: the long, slow, painstaking process of loosening an old system's restraints that hold our people captive. Being patient and courageous enough to pry open the spiderweb of cracks in the pyramid's walls, even if it endangers our tiny, powerful room at the top.

Notes

1   The phrase *great men,* in the context of leadership scholarship, originated in a time mostly blind to issues of gender discrimination. We use that phrase in this text as a historical reference, with awareness of its limitations and flaws.

2   Thomas Carlyle created the great-man theory of leadership through speeches and the book *On Heroes, Hero-Worship, and the Heroic in History,* published in 1841.

3   Yuval Levin, *A Time to Build: From Family and Community to Congress and the Campus, How Recommitting to Our Institutions Can Revive the American Dream* (New York: Basic Books, 2020), 37–38.

4   "Confidence in Institutions," Gallup, https://tinyurl.com/5n7er68m, accessed April 19, 2023.

5   We prefer a different set of three B's: believing, belonging, and becoming.

6   Gil Rendle, *Countercultural: Subversive Resistance and the Neighborhood Congregation* (Lanham, MD: Rowman & Littlefield, 2023), chap. 4, citing Robert Quinn.

7   Warren Bennis, foreword to Sharon Daloz Parks, *Leadership Can Be Taught: A Bold Approach for a Complex World* (Cambridge: Harvard Business School Press, 2005), ix.

8   Data cited from 2021. See Jeffrey M. Jones, "Confidence in U.S. Institutions Down; Average at New Low," Gallup, July 5, 2022, https://tinyurl.com/3nk4n638.

9   Garen J. Wintemute, Sonia Robinson, Andrew Crawford, Julia P. Schleimer, Amy Barnhorst, Vicka Chaplin, Daniel Tancredi, Elizabeth A. Tomsich, and Veronica A. Pear, "Views of American Democracy and Society and Support for Political Violence: First Report from a Nationwide Population-Representative Survey," preprint, July 19, 2022, https://tinyurl.com/4uvn2fyt.

10 The phrase "absolute power corrupts absolutely" is a selection from Lord Acton's letter to Bishop Creighton in 1887. As for the examples we have chosen, these are just three selected out of the widespread plague of abuse in religious life. We cite them with recognition that there are many other stories to tell. This book is not intended to offer a complete, ranked, or panoramic picture of religious abuse.

11 Elliot Bougis, "Pope Francis and the Papal Pyramid: Looking through the Wrong End of the Telescope," One Peter Five, October 26, 2015, https://tinyurl.com/bd9zcps.

12 Associated Press, "Top Southern Baptists Stonewalled and Denigrated Sex Abuse Victims, Report Says," NPR, May 22, 2022, https://tinyurl.com/kuu9zpmy.

13 Brian Planalp, "Report Details Decades of Sexual Harassment Allegations at Hebrew Union College," Fox 19 Now, November 19, 2021, https://tinyurl.com/43dhxmnc.

14 Jerry Useem, "Power Causes Brain Damage," *The Atlantic* (July/August 2017), https://tinyurl.com/3xa82kn5.

15 Useem, "Power Causes Brain Damage."

16 We would suggest that they become spiritually isolated as well.

17 From Howard Thurman's baccalaureate address at Spelman College, May 4, 1980, reprinted at https://www.uindy.edu/eip/files/reflection4.pdf.

18 Useem, "Power Causes Brain Damage."

19 Katayoun Kishi, "Key Findings on the Global Rise in Religious Restrictions," Pew Research Center, June 21, 2018, https://tinyurl.com/2s4235ju.

20 Kim's Twitter handle is @EugenePKim2 (this assumes—perhaps with too much faith—that Twitter will still be in existence by this book's publication date).

21 Eugene Kim, interview, August 16, 2022.

22 Kim, interview.

23 Nathan Aaseng, "Preacher Voice," Working Preacher, July 9, 2008, https://tinyurl.com/3rczk9vh. In the words of the author, "Preacher voice is similar to donning silk, ruffs, and powder. The formality does not enhance the message; it gets in the way. It changes me from a preacher into a caricature of a preacher."

24 Kim, interview.

25 Kim reflected during this Zoom interview that he happened at the time to be wearing black.

26 Kim, interview.

27 Kim, interview.

28 Kim, interview.

29 Kim, interview.

30 "2010 Church Consulting Future Trends Report," Church Consultation, 2010, https://tinyurl.com/49682vtc.

31 Kim, interview.

32 Joseph Campbell first identified and outlined the stages of the hero's journey in 1949 in his book *The Hero with a Thousand Faces*.

33 Baldwin and Linnea, *Circle Way*, 11.

34 Eugene Kim, email, November 11, 2022.

CHAPTER THREE

Breaking Free

A Liberation Project: Kathi's Story

The clergy intensive described in the prologue was designed for pastors leading their congregations' participation in the Changemaker Church Movement.[1] The Changemaker Church Movement is a Lilly Endowment–funded project designed to turn congregations toward a more innovative culture, reimagining their primary work as empowering laypeople to live as compassion-driven changemakers like Jesus.

The changemaker model for congregations flips on its head the traditional notion that many pastors have absorbed: that effective church leadership requires convincing congregants to focus less energy on their day jobs, family, and other commitments so that they can spend more of their resources participating in the activities and institutional priorities of their church. Instead, a changemaker church culture embraces the notion that laypeople's daily relationships *outside* the church are where faith becomes meaning making, where it is stretched and put into action.

The gospel finds its reflection (or not) every day—in workplaces, schools, neighborhoods, families. The church's most effective and most necessary work is to see, encourage, and honor the changemaking presence that laypeople bring with them into those places. Pastoral ministry's most essential function, I've begun to think, is not to convince them to chart a brand-new path that brings more focus and attention to the church. It's to empower people—to inspire, equip, and bless their investment in the lives they are already leading. It's the church saying to its people: How can the church support you in being part of God's changemaking, compassionate action in all the communities you are part of?[2]

Changemaker pastors listen more and talk less. They measure their effectiveness as pastors not by their own productivity or the church's institutional metrics but by the spiritually rooted, compassionate action of their laypeople—outside the church. This kind of shift necessarily brings a less tidy, more irregular shape to the activity of congregational life. In the changemaker church I led, I often felt like I was barely hanging onto the back of a bucking bronco. It was terrifying, to be sure, but also exhilarating.

I needed that rekindled sense of exhilaration as I entered the last years of my career in pastoral ministry. By many measures my ministry in the United Methodist Church had been fruitful. I led a series of increasingly large, diverse, and growth-oriented congregations. I could point to a few people in each whose lives had shifted toward transformation. In each church we added a few new programs that either held on for a while or didn't. I'd done more than my share of conference leadership work. But for the entire twenty-five years I was an active ordained pastor, the church continued in its decline. I often felt like I had my finger in a dike; all the cultural forces seemed aligned to topple the institution that held both our faith tradition and the measurement of my personal success. For years, I spent my Sunday mornings looking out at my congregation with my jaw clenched, as if I could conjure up more church attendance and volunteer energy by the sheer force of my concentration.

Pointing my congregation toward a different goal—creating a congregational culture that would equip people to live as compassion-driven changemakers in their lives outside the church—pulled the rug out from under me. So many of the leadership skills I'd learned to rely on were no longer relevant in this emerging work. If I was going to make my ministry about empowering other people, I had to learn to be more watchful about where the force of my personality, my confidence in my personal vision, and my intuitive sense of strategy crowded out other voices. I had to catch myself and back up when I naturally stepped to the front of the room. I had to risk our failing—my failing, in others' eyes—at some of the benchmarks that typically mark congregational success.

As it turns out, there were apostles of change who held this vision of ministry long before I figured it out for myself. In my focus on institutional leadership, I just hadn't heard them.

The Partial Truth behind the Pyramids

Widely accepted legends about great leaders are remarkably difficult to dislodge; they are stuck to the shadow of every frontrunner who rises through the ranks of organization and industry alike. They tell of superheroic efforts to overcome great obstacles, slay fearsome dragons, and never give up, even in the face of certain defeat. They celebrate the leaders who ignore the wise counsel of their mentors and the logical critique of their detractors. They advance an image of chosen leadership that is beyond the capacity of mere mortals.

These legends became widespread not only because they're entertaining and inspiring, or because they whisk our imaginations to far-off lands and outlandish possibilities for this one protagonist. They stay with us because those legends are at least partially true. There's enough documented truth in the success stories of singularly skilled leaders to draw us all in. Sometimes it does take a herculean effort by one individual to lead a community through trying times. Sometimes the moment calls for a certain expertise, courage, or wisdom held by one—and only one—person. The Israelites might still be in Egypt if Moses didn't eventually accept God's charge, or be stuck on the shores of the Red Sea if Nachshon didn't take those first brave steps,[3] or have given up completely if Miriam didn't initially pack the tambourines so she could lift their spirits with song. In other words, it's more complicated than we think.[4]

The empire simultaneously captivates us and leads us to believe that we can break its spell. That is why the following group of modern-day prophets—those who have challenged the status quo, at personal and professional risk—stand out so sharply from the rest.

The Word of the Prophets, Then and Now

There is a long tradition of observers who have intermittently been brave enough to poke and provoke the leaders of even the most fortified institutions. In the ancient stories of our faith tradition, prophets were dispatched by God to speak wisdom that countered, and sometimes defied, Israel's kings. Samuel, Nathan, Jeremiah, Amos—each of them dared to remind a powerful monarch that their power was not absolute, that they were accountable to something other than their own agenda, and sometimes that their behavior had gone off track. The presence of God in the world is alive and active, those prophets declared to even the most popular leaders. You are not its complete expression.

Today's prophets of change are less likely to claim divine backing. They speak in the language of management wisdom, human capacity, and sometimes a vague spirituality. Their arguments tend to speak more of productivity than of sacred purpose. But their voices carry to institutional leaders a message not unlike the biblical prophets' warning to kings. The walls of our organizational pyramids, they say, are not so smooth and unperturbed as we once thought. There is disruption work to be done.

From the American business community, too, a deep well of secular voices suggests a more generous alternative to the pyramid-shaped culture present everywhere in organizational life. These practical prophets offer alternatives to the great-man theory of leadership. The power that great leaders have historically held, they say, is meant to be shared, not hoarded. Collections of people can make things happen, but not when they're entombed in pyramids. We need organizational formations that invite agency and voice from persons in every position.

These agitators are not always loud, but they have been persistent. The most effective leadership, they say, is inclusive, respectful, and just. The ultimate point of leadership is not to impose a single voice and vision but to collectively breathe life into a broadly shared, living body of wisdom. The most effective leader is one who knows when he or she is *not* necessary. Each of these countercultural voices echoes the surprising proposition of the Gospel story: like loaves and fishes, power multiplies when it is shared. And while these prophets' experiments have yielded as many failures as successes, their ideas continue to provoke.

Charles A. Coffin

The first president of General Electric, Charles A. Coffin, led that company for twenty years, from its founding in 1892. Coffin knew almost nothing about electric lighting when he took over leadership of the struggling company. He had been until then a shoemaker, modest in his ambition and achievements. He knew the company's success depended on the mastery of employees throughout General Electric's ranks, at every level of the company's operations. He called every employee, from executive to the most junior assembly line operator, "my associate." He invited line laborers to think for themselves, to exercise their own judgment in their work, and to propose entrepreneurial ideas as soon as they came to mind, bureaucracy be damned. Workers were encouraged to create their own products and to test them using company resources.[5] Under Coffin's leadership, General Electric became enormously successful by many measures. But one of its most noted accomplishments was General Electric's development of a system of management that offered equal dignity to every person and space for every employee's ingenuity to contribute to the company's mission.

Coffin shows up as number one on Jim Collins's 2003 list of the ten greatest CEOs of all time. Collins writes, "While [Thomas] Edison [the inventor behind General Electric's success] was essentially a genius with a thousand helpers, Coffin created a system of genius that did not depend on him."[6] General Electric's corporate biographer writes, "No man exercised his leadership with greater simplicity, greater humility, greater regard for others. . . . He dominated, it is true; but he never domineered. His dominance sprang directly from the confidence which others placed in him."[7]

Mary Parker Follett

Mary Parker Follett was born in 1868 outside Boston. While she was a student at the Annex at Harvard (later renamed Radcliffe College), she studied under the psychologist and philosopher William James, the founder of the philosophical tradition of pragmatism. Pragmatism suggests that the significance of our convictions is demonstrated by their influence on what we do. Truth derives not from some independent principle, tradition, or authority, but in the impact, the fruits, of our actions. Love, trust, and personal respect—the principles we often associate with religious integrity—are also pragmatic values. They are virtuous, pragmatists say, not because a divine authority spoke them into being but because of the positive effect they have on other people and on our communities. The entire ethos of civility and humanity that is critical to American democracy,

James said, depends on the tone we set in our personal and civic relationships.[8]

Follett extended James's philosophy of pragmatism into the realm of organizational effectiveness. In a book published from her graduate thesis, she argues that leaders build strong organizations by nurturing the collective power of the organization's members or employees. The organization's mission is furthered, and its power enhanced, she says, by engaging the active, creative contributions of workers at every level of the organization's life. Shared power is not only virtuous; it generates a more potent leadership than either personal charisma or command exercised from the top.

Follett tested her theory first in social-reform work. She went to work with women who had volunteered to welcome immigrants to Boston. Serving the newcomers would not equip them to be citizens, Follett convinced those volunteers. So they began to encourage the agency of the immigrants themselves—organizing a debate club, developing job training, and arranging for public school facilities to be available as community gathering places. Follett advocated for housing communities where volunteer leaders and the immigrants they were serving could live side by side. These innovations changed the shape and nature of the work. Its purpose shifted; it was not merely to serve but to empower the newly arrived immigrants. Everyone's voice mattered; every contribution counted in a broad collective of effort and mutual respect.

What Follett saw had implications beyond volunteerism and the "women's work" of her era. Gradually, she extended her ideas toward corporate enterprise. She proposed that interdependence created the energy critical to business success. Groups of people working together, she suggested, could develop a capacity that exceeded the power of even the most capable leader. She advocated for work in teams, inviting every member to offer ideas and opinions from whatever position they held in the corporate structure. She lectured on the art of "power-with" rather than "power-over" others.

By the mid-1920s, Follett had become an influential voice among corporate executives. Business behemoths such as General Motors, AT&T, and R. H. Macy Company demonstrated openness to adjustments in their corporate culture to encourage internal interdependence. And then, in 1929, the stock market crashed. Anxiety reigned. And the pyramid reasserted itself and returned to unquestioned prominence.

Stephen R. Covey

In 1989, Stephen R. Covey's book *The Seven Habits of Highly Effective People* splashed into American organizational consciousness. Echoing Follett's work decades earlier, Covey posited that the most effective leaders foster interdependence—mutual respect and purposeful connection. People who are highly effective in both business and personal life, he said, propose win-win solutions to problems, listen to others with empathy, and lean on teamwork rather than trying to make themselves into an island of excellence.

Covey's book was enormously influential on businesses as well as individuals. The book sold over twenty-five million copies. It was translated into fifty-two languages. It was an early entry in a new industry of self-help books, courses, and TED talks; it captured a wisdom that felt spiritual as well as professional. It sparked a product line of posters and desktop tchotchkes that borrow inspiration from Thomas Merton as faithfully as they do from Peter Drucker, often melding the two. "Management is efficiency in climbing the ladder of success. Leadership determines whether the ladder is leaning against the right wall."[9]

Fifteen years after the publication of *Seven Habits*, Covey published an addendum. In *The Eighth Habit*, Covey returns to the idea of interdependence. He underlines and expands on the importance of building trust and mutual empowerment as a practice for effective, soulful leadership. The necessary eighth habit of leadership lies beyond intellect, competence, and decisiveness. In culturally palatable language, Covey offers readers a version of the spiritual transformation religion has long pointed toward. A thoughtful leader seeking professional success will—in fact, must—find compassion and humility along the way.

Jim Collins

Jim Collins's *Good to Great*, published in 2001, caught a similarly captivating wave of reflection on organizational leadership. As he analyzed the factors that make the difference between companies that sustain greatness and those identified by short-term financial success, Collins created a vocabulary that, two decades later, still influences leadership practice in almost every kind of organization. Getting the right people on the bus, the hedgehog concept, the flywheel effect—these are now common catchphrases in management circles. Great leaders, he said, are not necessarily "great men." Great organizations are led by what he describes as a *level-five leader.*

Like most ambitious leaders, level-five leaders are intensely determined and deeply invested in their own success and in their organization's performance. What distinguishes a level-five leader, Collins writes, is not charisma or skill or even vision; it's character. Level-five leaders aren't larger than life or self-aggrandizing; they're humble, modest, even understated. They put their tremendous professional will to work not for personal reward or ascent but to catalyze and nurture the energy of a wide set of contributors to their organization's mission. They trust associates and employees to do their work well; in turn, their subordinates trust them enough to risk bringing their ideas and opinions to the table. That broad engagement throughout the organization—that interdependence—is the difference between great organizations and flashes in the pan.

Joseph Raelin

At around the same time as the publication of *Good to Great*, the educator and scholar Joseph Raelin proposed an alternative model, not only for leaders but for entire organizations.[10] Expanding on the work of the management consultant and writer Margaret Wheatley and others, Raelin proposed an organizational arrangement he called *leaderful*. Leadership, he wrote, is a collective, collaborative enterprise. Leaderful organizations improve their productivity and life together not by training better followers but by making room for more leaders.

Every day, Raelin wrote, an organization's decisions require knowledge in the possession of workers who have lower positions and sometimes very little authority in the organizational hierarchy. Those workers—whether teachers in classrooms, military personnel on the ground, assembly-line workers, or grocery clerks—take actions that advance the organization's mission through commitment and cohesion. The most effective organizations encourage each of these subordinates to generate energy from their own sense of mission and to act on their own authority rather than depending on specific direction from above. These organizations are not leaderless, Raelin wrote; they are leader*ful*.

In Raelin's design, leaderful organizations are shaped like circles, not triangles. Leadership emerges from any location, not just from some uppermost peak. Every employee or member of the organization must be empowered not just to follow directions and not just to support the decisions of a single leader or manager, but to craft their own work to cohere with the rest of the organization's project.

Twenty-First-Century Movements

New Power

Raelin's perspective never became a predominant view, but twenty-first-century technology has accelerated his argument.

Social media allows everyone—not just a select, chosen few—to influence the actions of others. We have a new definition of followers now; that description signals enthusiasm, not necessarily obedience. Jeremy Heimans and Henry Timms's book *New Power* says it this way:

> **Old power** works *like a currency.* It is held by few. Once gained, it is jealously guarded, and the powerful have a substantial store of it to spend. It is closed, inaccessible, and leader-driven. It downloads, and it captures.
>
> **New power** operates differently, *like a current.* It is made by many. It is open, participatory, and peer-driven. It uploads, and it distributes. Like water or electricity, it's most forceful when it surges. The goal with new power is not to hoard it but to channel it.[11]

Something in the culture has shifted, these authors say. New power is already widely shared. Influence does not depend on a position or title conferred by an organization, or on any external authority; it ebbs and flows with its own unrestricted current. The wave of new power reached tidal proportions in the postpandemic Great Resignation and a generation of workers who quietly quit their day jobs. But this restlessness started long before Covid. Americans began transferring their search for purpose and transcendence from worship to work a long time ago.[12] In 2014, more than half (53 percent) of millennial respondents said having their passions and talents recognized and addressed is their top reason for remaining at their current company, the *New Power* authors report.[13] Today, jobs do more than pay the bills; they have to provide fulfillment on a daily basis, too. When workers are undervalued, underutilized, or overwhelmed with busywork, they resist powerfully. They have little tolerance for being instrumentalized, seen for anything less than their full potential. This is their new power: "a new expectation: an inalienable right to participate."[14]

Holacracy

In 2015, a successful start-up entrepreneur named Brian Robertson launched a small movement with a book called *Holacracy: The New Management System for a Rapidly Changing World*. Robertson's TEDx talk proposed "a revolutionary management system that redefines management and turns everyone into a leader."[15] Power is not a limited resource, Robertson argued, and distributing power does not necessarily lead to undisciplined anarchy. Holacracy proposes that businesses put in place a negotiated constitution establishing a clear set of organizational roles and mutually respectful boundaries around every position. It imagines a well-defined, flattened structure that allows individuals and teams to self-manage—to make decisions, organize their work, serve customers, and resolve problems that come up along the way

Holacracy made a splashy entrance into the world of leadership practice. It had a few high-profile practitioners, most visibly the shoe-sales company Zappos and its founding CEO, the late Tony Hsieh. Zappos famously focused on its workplace culture and on employee satisfaction. "We want our employees to find meaning in their work," an executive told a *Forbes* reporter in 2017.[16] Team members are given freedom to act outside their box; leaders set their teams up for success by stepping out of the way. In theory, at least, every call-center representative knows they have all the tools and discretion they need to make customers happy—to do their job completely. They don't need to ask a supervisor for permission to override policies or compensate for lapses in service.

The reward holacracy promised was significant and compelling: power invested in every employee to innovate and make changes, freedom to exercise their own judgment and creativity. But with great power comes great responsibility; the demands holacracy places on employees are quite high. Working together this way requires empathy, compassion, healthy communication, and the personal maturity of workers at every level of the organization's life. Holacracy promises that organizational systems can be constructed to build those capacities through rules and processes, checks and balances, guidelines that avoid overstepping. But maintaining this structure is labor- and attention-intensive. The correlation between workers' self-actualization and efficient accomplishment of the company's business purpose is sometimes elusive.[17]

The Power of Giving Away Power

In 2021, the ambassador, serial entrepreneur, and political operative Matthew Barzun published *The Power of Giving Away Power*. With illustrations as varied as the founding of American democracy, the pattern of fractals in nature, and the 2008 presidential campaign of Barack Obama, Barzun calls into question the pyramid mindset that dominates Western culture. His metaphor is the US dollar bill, which bears the image of the ancient pyramids. The reference to pyramid-shaped power, he says, was intentional. That symbol was consciously chosen as the new nation turned away from its origins as a loose constellation of thirteen states and deliberately took on the architecture of empire.

The pyramid mindset is useful for nation building, Barzun argues; it plans away uncertainty, trades individual power for the higher priority of simplification and single-mindedness; it commends stability above all else.[18] But the pyramid also dehumanizes its occupants. It privileges the voices of those who speak command and control from a higher position as it silences all the rest. It prizes engagement with each other in limited ways; it works best when each of us regards ourselves as our functions, stripped of the variations of human temperament. But when we opt for unmitigated orderliness, certainty, and efficiency, there is a cost: the resourcefulness of communities, the thriving of workers and citizens, the humanity of leaders. The pyramid sacrifices, for the sake of driven, single-minded purpose, the blessings of relationship, the infinite possibility and power of us together.

Each of these movements is an exploration into new configurations of leadership. All of them embody a persistent restlessness, recognition that the powers of creativity and resourcefulness are not meagerly distributed or reserved for a select few. Their urgings sound spiritual even when they arise from decidedly secular contexts. Practical prophets and movement observers echo the warnings of ancient prophets, who pointed out cracks long before their empires' buildings started to crumble. Maybe the repeated swells of an insistent human agency will finally disturb the stubborn stability of the ancient, rigid structures that have held us—leaders and underlings alike—inside our stifling pyramids.

Movement of the Spirit

Leading with integrity is not a technique; it's a character issue. It calls for an internalized set of values embedded more deeply than the short-term imperative for fortune or success that drives both religious and nonreligious organizations. The work is internal, and it is profound. Even the voices of secular prophets who have called for new models of leadership stretch toward values we recognize as spiritual.

Collins's analysis of level-five leaders observed a trend: life-changing experiences with cancer, brushes with accidental death, and strong religious beliefs, sometimes even a conversion experience, had prepared them for evolved leadership.[19] Raelin lists attentive listening, humility, inner peace, and a joyful spirit as "leaderful values."[20] Holacracy founder Robertson describes his system as "a stealth spiritual . . . transformative practice."[21] *New Power* authors Heimans and Timms turn to Pope Francis frequently to illustrate their argument for institutional transformation, calling him a "walking parable," admiring the visible signs of his humility, his urging for the church to invert its own pyramid.[22] Barzun uses similarly spiritual language. He closes his argument for shared power systems with the story of President Barack Obama's decision to risk vulnerability as he began to sing "Amazing Grace" at a memorial service in Charleston, South Carolina.

> His [Obama's] singing was . . . well . . . let's say good but not great. But he met the congregation halfway and they were there for him. It was freedom together that helped heal a sorrowful president, congregation, and nation. He had the power of the pulpit and the microphone and the position and place, and he gave away that power to the congregation. And in so doing, a bloom loop sprung out of [an] awkward thirteen seconds [when he sang alone]. Individuals jumped in, joining their voices with Obama's. The congregants needed Obama, but maybe they were surprised to learn that he had come in expecting to need them too. All were changed.[23]

People of faith have heard these messages before. In the effectiveness-framed language of business-leadership advice, we hear a prophetic invocation of values that religious traditions have long spoken for, an echo of the divine impulse toward freedom that initiated the Hebrew slaves' exodus from Egypt. Perhaps we are hearing again God's "I have seen the oppression of my people" (Exod 3:7), addressing the constricting shape of the pyramid. Its structure may be stable, it may employ workers and resources efficiently, but it does not facilitate human flourishing.

Religious Leadership Is Different (Or Is It?)

Parallel to this strand of secular prophets, faith-based and faith-adjacent writers offer religious leaders another body of guidance. Their wisdom rests explicitly on an alternative set of values we might think of as spiritual: generosity, authenticity, other-centered humility. Many of these strands of leadership wisdom are familiar: adaptive leadership, transformative leadership, collaborative leadership, servant leadership, nonanxious leadership.[24] In increasingly insistent metaphors, congregational leaders have been encouraged to canoe the mountains, examine our motives, and accept the relocation of our pulpits to off-center.[25] The array of wisdom is bountiful, even dizzying.

Conscientious leaders of religious organizations have to work hard to keep up with this parade of leadership advice. There is always one more new program, another novel improvement to try. In the meantime, the work of holding up an institution heavy with its own traditions gets progressively harder. It takes more time and effort just to stay in place. The gains we make are fragile and temporary. We are running in place, exhausting ourselves trying to rally the small but faithful remnant against an undertow of cultural resistance. The tide is draining their energy faster than our small buckets can possibly pour it in.

But what if the execution of wise, life-giving, coherent leadership isn't as complicated as the intricate web of leadership theories can sometimes make it seem? What if it is simply not true that thriving communities require an assemblage of astounding gifts in one extraordinary leader?

The most effective *and* the most faithful leadership does not require more charisma or skill or confidence. It takes knowing, trusting, acting on what is no doubt true: that the people you lead have a vast, unmined capacity to lead with you, alongside you, maybe even ahead of you. Your work—your most essential work—is to unlock the door to the small room in which their gifts have been confined. To set them free.

Breaking Free: Eugene Kim's Story Continued

Stepping out of the pyramid was not an easy process for Eugene Kim. The path forward was never all that clear, the obstacles along the way sometimes felt insurmountable, and success was never guaranteed. He expected no miracles to light his way; there was no promise of manna sitting on the table to feed his family. He wasn't sure there was a promised land waiting for his arrival.

In his first few months after leaving the church, Kim committed himself almost entirely to listening. He spent time with young people who felt disenfranchised by church or who had already left the church. Some told him they had left because they felt that the church didn't welcome them as they were, some because their experiences at church felt more like a spectator sport than a soulful connection with the divine. Others moved on because they wanted to feel a deeper sense of ownership over their spiritual lives, and church seemed to run by a different idea.

He also listened intently to his peers in professional ministry, many of whom had burned out, stepped away for a time, or left faith leadership completely. There, too, he picked up on some common threads. Some of them came to realize that bigger was not in fact better. They yearned to go back into small, intimate communities. Some had grown exhausted after years of overfunctioning, finding in themselves feelings of resentment toward congregants who were growing more passive with each passing year. And others had come to see that their main project as a church leader was simply to survive. They found themselves in the business of staying in business, and that was not where they wanted to be.

Kim also listened to his inner voice. He reflected on the remarkable run he'd had in church leadership. He'd helped build a thriving church community. But the personal, professional, and spiritual costs of operating within the church's power structure had been high. As he gained greater clarity, he knew he didn't want to replicate the same pyramid, even if he were the one sitting at its top. A vision for the future started to take shape. A very different shape, in fact.

New Wineskins

A student of Anna Linnea's and Christina Baldwin's *The Circle Way*, Kim began to explore the notion of building a community of communities, each designed in the simple, humble shape of a circle. He was powerfully drawn to the possibility of building an organization that was framed entirely by the equity and mutuality implied by a circle's shape. "The shape itself offers many benefits. Circle is the form of endlessness, continuation, calming down, pacifying. In a circle, there's no beginning or end—once you're in the circle, you're there, participating in wholeness. Nobody is superior; no one is better than anyone else. We sit together in our differences in one nice, round shape."[26]

After a quarter-century in church leadership, wrestling with his own feelings of internal dissonance and disenfranchisement, Kim longed to participate in something that embodied and invited wholeness—his and others'. He remembered his first calling: to respond to people's need for a community that would invite them in, no matter where in the world they laid their head at night, no matter what their past experiences had been, and no matter how they wanted to show up. And that's exactly what Kim and his team have built.

The founding team for the New Wine Collective was captured early on by a scriptural metaphor that represented much of what they wanted to manifest in the world. Jesus said that wise people "do not pour new wine into old wineskins . . . they pour new wine into new wineskins" (Matt 9:17). The metaphor spoke deeply to Kim and his partners' shared yearning to build an entirely new model—one where new wine flowed not only from the appointed leader but from everyone around the circle. It would also be one where the new wineskins into which it flowed freely were held equitably by those same folks around the circle. Every person in the circle would be liberated to hold, interpret, and enact the insight that came to them.

Once the framework for their new venture was established, the name—New Wine Collective—followed quickly. Kim says,

> New Wine represents the radically new spirituality Christ embodied that transcended and challenged the religious structures of his day. New wine requires *new wineskins*—new forms and practices that serve as containers for a new way of relating to God, to one another, and to the world. A Collective is a group of people working toward a common goal or purpose that does not rely on internal established hierarchies. In a collective, leadership is flexible, shared, and collaborative.[27]

The purpose of the New Wine Collective rests on the clarity of the prophetic challenge Kim and his partners have heard: to love the world as it is, while holding it together with a vision for the world as it could be. The invitation is as simple as a circle, he says: New Wine Collective is for all the folks religious organizations are losing—the ones who left church or never went in the first place, the pastors who stepped away and haven't looked back. It's for "seekers, skeptics, and spiritual misfits looking for an alternative to traditional forms of organized religion."[28]

> It's very simple, not ingenious at all. If we just take turns and if we create a community in which every voice matters, that's a far more healthy expression of humanity and belonging than what I grew up with. . . . I think that's the shape of real community. It's not one part dominating the others, but there is a flow, and every voice matters in a community that is mutual and respects each individual's autonomy.[29]

The idea stays as simple as it began: to bring strangers together from all around the world to share scriptural wisdom in their own words, in their own contexts, on their own time. Just three actions ground all the rest of the collective's work: equip, entrust, and empower. The technology is sophisticated: it involves a software platform, with some fairly complex coding. This facilitates the sharing of knowledge and mindful awareness of each location's unique culture, values, and communication styles among a growing community of diverse communities. But technology is the medium, not the message; it provides only the platform for people to connect regularly with one another as teacher and student, gatherer and gathered. Every small community finds its own way to live into the core values of the collective, and each is empowered to explore where those values lead.

Keeping It Simple

As Kim disciplines himself to practice the countercultural leadership required for this model, he reflects back on the struggles of his earlier life in ministry and the complex power dynamics he faced in the pulpit. There is boundless potential in the New Wineskins model, the possibility of almost limitless growth. But he knows that both his own healing and avoiding similar damage to others require attentiveness, resisting the too-easy metamorphosis into the geometry of a pyramid. Kim turns back to his teachers-through-text, Baldwin and Linnea, authors of *The Circle Way*:

> We have the opportunity . . . to heal our old stories and to make new stories that lead to different actions and create a different world. This is the essential task of our times! Understanding the power of story and the container of the circle give us life skills that have profoundly transformational potential. We can talk the world we need into being and then align our actions with our vision. This is what our ancestors did at the fire, and if we are to become ancestors to future generations, this is what we will do today.[30]

Remarkable leaders like Kim are imagining new forms of faith community and new models of leadership. We won't all be entrepreneurial founders of new technology platforms, but every leader is capable of asking hard questions of the systems we've inherited, new and old. Questions such as, Does the shape of your organization elevate the giftedness of every person, including yourself? Do the patterns of your leadership make room for everyone to contribute and grow? In the story of your organization's work, who are the heroes, and what must they overcome?

▲

Stepping into the Deep:
Moses's Story

Finally, the obstacles are cleared; the furtive preparations are made. In one frenetic night, the Israelites gather up small packages of their most necessary belongings, a few pieces of jewelry either borrowed or stolen from their Egyptian neighbors, pans of unleavened bread—just enough. They will have to bake it later, in the sun. And the Israelites simply walk away from their enslavement. There is no explanation for the Egyptians' last-minute forbearance, other than a Pharaoh who has simply had enough of the havoc wrought by the God of these troublesome slaves.

For 430 years the Israelites have lived and worked at the foot of the pyramids. They will have to walk a long way before they leave behind the shadow of those monstrous structures. They come to the edge of the sea and camp there. They pause to offer thanks, no doubt mentioning prominently their leader, Moses, who has heroically led them into a miraculous escape. And then they hear, faintly, the distant thunder of hooves and chariots, the clatter of military equipment. They look up and realize they are trapped, between a humiliated army and an immovable ocean.

Moses is at first unshaken. Surely God will prop up his leadership again, intervene to bolster Moses's control over this situation. God will destroy the Egyptians or transport the Israelites safely across the Reed Sea. Surely all the people have to do is stand by and observe another manifestation of divine power.

Moses deepens his voice and commands the restless and fearful people. "Don't be afraid. Watch! God will deliver you." But he too is afraid. He lowers his head, conceals his anxiety in prayer. The people stand still, expectantly, at the edge of the sea. Nothing happens. The galloping grows louder. Finally, God's voice comes to Moses. "Why are you crying out to me? Tell the Israelites to get moving!" Moses opens one eye. Who heard this word that held the unmistakable sound of a rebuke? And where are they supposed to move?

But not everyone is frozen in place. The midrash, the stories and interpretations that have gathered over centuries of tradition, tell that in the crowd that day there is one person who sees what needs to be done. It is Nachshon ben Aminadav, head of the tribe of Judah. Perhaps Nachshon senses Moses's hesitation. Maybe he sees panic in the eyes of the Israelites. Or maybe he has always been impulsive. Whatever it is, Nachshon does not wait for Moses to regather his resources or draw up a new strategy. He steps off the bank and walks straight into the water (Mechilta d'Rabbi Yishmael 14:22).

The midrashic storytellers have imagined what happened next, what follows the moment when one leader hesitates and another—so far unnamed in the exodus story—steps forward. They say that the people followed Nachshon into the still-foaming water. His bravery has inspired them; they are ready to sacrifice their own lives. They wade in; the water rises past their knees, their waists, their shoulders. It is not until the waves reach their nostrils that the waters begin to stand aside. Only when the people have committed themselves to the path on which God has led them can Moses's miracle take effect. The necessary faith is not just the leader's; the people, too, must be up to their noses in risk before the waters will divide to make a way for the Israelites' watery escape.[31]

Other midrashic stories imagine that Nachshon floundered as he reached deep water. He begins to drown. Moses can see what is happening; he is afraid that others will follow Nachshon into certain death. He cries out to God again. "Save him!" Again God hands back to Moses the responsibility for action. "Your people are drowning, the sea is closing in on him, the enemy is in close pursuit, and you stand there praying? You do something!"[32]

Perhaps God can see that the situation is getting away from the ill-equipped leader; God proffers a more specific direction to Moses. "And you lift up your rod and hold out your arm over the sea and split it" (Exod 14:16). A double measure of power is invoked: the staff that symbolizes the presence and power of God, the hand that belongs to a human leader. Moses holds out his rod and his hand both; the waters part. The people walk safely to the other side of the sea, on dry ground.

One thing is clear: the crossing of the sea is not Moses's miracle alone. It is not even Moses's and God's together. In this early wilderness experience, Moses must see that it will not always be his willful, singular leadership that opens a way forward. It is not his example alone that will call the people into action.

Who is this Nachshon, who stepped out of his place in the crowd without invitation and whose impulsive bravery propelled him to the front at a critical moment? Moses will turn to Nachshon again. He will depend again on Nachshon's untapped capability during this wilderness journey. In the meantime, as he walks behind over the dry floor of this tunnel whose walls are water, Moses must wonder: What does it mean, this moment when another stepped forward and he stepped back?

Has his authority been usurped? Should he feel inadequate, even shamed? Or has the singular burden of responsibility for this journey to freedom been lifted from his shoulders?

Notes

1 See www.thechangemakerinitiative.org.
2 See more about the Changemaker Initiative in Kenda Creasy Dean, *Innovating for Love: Joining God's Initiative through Christian Social Innovation* (Knoxville, TN: Market Square, 2022).
3 Midrash Exodus Rabbah 13.
4 Credit to the inimitable Rabbi Brad Hirschfield for first teaching Elan that just about everything is "more complicated than we think."
5 "Charles A. Coffin," The Leadership of General Electric, August 7, 2019, https://tinyurl.com/mz3dkhmc.
6 Jim Collins, "The 10 Greatest CEOs of All Time," *Fortune*, July 21, 2003, https://tinyurl.com/2s444dnk.
7 John Hammond, *Men and Volts: The Story of General Electric*, cited in Jed Graham, "Charles Coffin, the Man Who Electrified GE," Investor's Business Daily, January 20, 2011, https://tinyurl.com/y2d6h4bv. Not every General Electric CEO who came later shared Coffin's philosophy of leadership. General Electric remained one of the country's most successful companies for almost a hundred years more, but some of its more recent leaders have modeled themselves as "great men" whose personal vision, drive, and firm hold on the top spot in the corporate pyramid have redefined the company's culture.
8 Matthew Barzun, *The Power of Giving Away Power* (New York: Random House, 2021), 52.
9 Stephen R. Covey, *The Seven Habits of Highly Effective People* (New York: Simon & Schuster 1989), 101, drawing from Trappist monk Thomas Merton's quote, "People may spend their whole lives climbing the ladder of success only to find, once they reach the top, that the ladder is leaning against the wrong wall."
10 Joseph Raelin, *Creating Leaderful Organizations* (Oakland, CA: Berrett-Koehler, 2003).
11 Heimans and Henry, *New Power*, 2.
12 Employers have made subtle and overt attempts at incorporating spirituality into the workplace for at least three decades. See Theology of Work Project, www.theologyofwork.org; Derek Thompson, "Workism Is Making Americans Miserable," *The Atlantic*, February 24, 2019, https://tinyurl.com/4vhej4dc; and Kathryn Post, "The

Dangers of Finding Meaning at Work," Religion News Service, June 8, 2022, https://tinyurl.com/2y9cjvu8.

13 Heimans and Timms, *New Power*, 225.

14 Heimans and Timms, *New Power*, 18.

15 Brian J. Robertson, *Holacracy: The New Management System for a Rapidly Changing World* (New York: Holt, 2015).

16 Chris Cancialosi, "Preserving a Culture People Love as Your Company Grows: Lessons from Zappos," *Forbes*, May 30, 2017, https://tinyurl.com/3nm8s3kb.

17 "How We Work," Zappos, https://www.zappos.com/about/how-we-work, accessed July 5, 2023.

18 Matthew Barzun, *The Power of Giving Away Power: How the Best Leaders Learn to Let Go* (San Francisco: HarperCollins, 2021), 135.

19 Jim Collins, *Good to Great: Why Some Companies Make the Leap and Others Don't* (San Francisco: HarperBusiness, 2001), 37.

20 Raelin, *Creating Leaderful Organizations*, 230.

21 Brian Robertson, "Holocracy: An Emergent Order System," *Kosmos* (Fall 2019), https://tinyurl.com/bdf47xxj.

22 Heimans and Timms, *New Power*, 173–77.

23 Barzun, *Power of Giving Away Power*, 194.

24 Ronald A. Heifetz, Marty Linsk, Alexander Grashow, *The Practice of Adaptive Leadership* (Cambridge: Harvard Business Press, 2009); Eloy Anello, Joan Hernandez, and May Khadem, *Transformative Leadership: Developing the Hidden Dimension* (self-pub., 2014); Peter M. DeWitt, *Collaborative Leadership: Six Influences That Matter Most* (Thousand Oaks, CA: Corwin, 2016); Robert K. Greenleaf, *Servant Leadership: A Journey into the Nature of Legitimate Power and Greatness* (Mahwah, NJ: Paulist, 1977); Edwin H. Friedman, *A Failure of Nerve: Leadership in the Age of the Quick Fix*, rev. ed. (New York: Church Publishing, 2017).

25 Tod S. Bolsinger, *Canoeing the Mountains: Christian Leadership in Uncharted Territory* (Downers Grove, IL: InterVarsity, 2018); Patrick M. Lencioni, *The Motive: Why So Many Leaders Abdicate Their Most Important Responsibilities* (San Francisco: Jossey-Bass, 2020); Thom S. Rainer, *Who Moved My Pulpit?: Leading Change in the Church* (Nashville: B&H Books, 2016). There is a helpful summary of recent church leader resources at https://tinyurl.com/z78j3nbw.

26 Baldwin and Linnea, *Circle Way*, x.

27 Eugene Kim, "Our Name & Logo," New Wine Collective, https://tinyurl.com/4f6hster, accessed December 8, 2022.

28 "Our Mission," New Wine Collective, https://tinyurl.com/mr3u6ujv, accessed November 30, 2022.

29 Kim, interview.

30 Baldwin and Linnea, *Circle Way*, 144.

31 Shemot Rabbah 21:9, note 34, in Avivah Gottlieb Zornberg, *The Particulars of Rapture: Reflections on Exodus* (repr., New York: Schocken, 2011), 516.

32 Paraphrased from b. Sotah 37a.

CHAPTER FOUR

The Way Up Is Down

There is a gaping chasm between embracing the idea of changing our behavior and putting real change into practice. The most important lessons of our lives must be learned again and again; we only gradually absorb the truth that the way we have always done things is not working. We realize slowly that it's not always other people who are responsible when our efforts are ineffective. Something in us is equally responsible for obstructing the path between our good intentions and the difference we had hoped to make. In Portia Nelson's powerful poem "Autobiography in Five Short Chapters," it takes her all five chapters (i.e., her whole life) to learn from the mistake she first makes in chapter 1. The pattern of a growing, self-reflective life is not a continuous ascent; it is falling down and standing up again, and again, and again.[1] That's true for everyone, especially those who seek lead others.

New Leader, Old Lament: Elan's Story

When I began my first assignment as a rabbi at a large synagogue, one of the first changes I made was to move my office hours from my temple office, which welcomed very little foot traffic during the week, to a local coffee shop nearby. I figured that it would send an important message to the community—that my goal was to meet them where they were, not expect them to come to me. Also, I love coffee, and this particular place offered free refills.

Twice a week, I would buy a cup of coffee and sit down at a table by the door to study Talmud. I never made it too far into my Talmud study. Just as I had hoped, folks would come in, notice the *kippah* on my head,[2] and approach me with a variation on one of two introductions:

"Are you the new rabbi? (Yes.) Great! Can we talk about (fill in the blank)?" or "Are you a rabbi? (Guilty as charged.) Well, I'm a bad Jew. (What do you mean by that?) I don't really believe in the fire-and-brimstone, old-man-in-the-sky God, and I definitely don't like sitting through long prayer services. (Well, in that case, you're in good company. Want to join me here and talk more?)"

One day, about three months into my tenure, one of these coffee-shop conversations took a completely different tone. Anne (not her real name), carrying a loaf of bread under her arm and in a hurry to get out to her car, did a double-take when she saw the *kippah* on my head. She walked over to me and asked, "Are you the new rabbi?" I smiled, thinking I knew where this was going, and cheerfully replied, "Yes, I am!" Her next sentences were not what I'd anticipated. "Well, I want you to know that I read the article about all the new stuff you're doing at the synagogue. You sound like a perfectly nice guy, but I'll never step foot in that place. Not after how they treated my son." I closed my volume of Talmud, slid my coffee to the side of the table, and gestured for her to take the empty chair across from me. She proceeded to tell me a story about bringing her son, who was a young adult at this point, to the synagogue about a decade prior. Her story broke my heart into pieces.

Diagnosed with autism at a young age, Anne's son had struggled for years to find a Jewish community where he would be welcomed with open arms. Over the years, their family bounced around from one house of worship to the next. The last place they tried was my new synagogue. When she had entered the sanctuary on a Saturday morning for services, she was overjoyed to watch her son warm up to the space quickly, dancing along to the music and singing along to the prayers as he could. After years of searching, it felt like they had finally found a Jewish home.

But before she could let her guard down and enjoy the moment, the scene unfolded as it so often does. As her son sang and danced boisterously to the prayers, Anne noticed a number of congregants turning around to find the source of the disruption. Some of them glared, others shushed. The message was clear: regardless of the "All are welcome!" sign prominently located in front of the building, families like hers were not really welcome. When staff and clergy reached out later to apologize and try to invite them back, the damage was already done. It was too late.

By the time Anne finished her story, we were both in tears. I thanked her for her honesty and vulnerability. I asked whether she would be willing to meet with me again. She reluctantly agreed, and soon enough we began a journey of three years of working closely together to build a new community of families and children with special needs. What she didn't know when she started her story was that this particular issue—special-needs inclusion—was one of the driving passions of my life. As a teen, I'd been part of the founding team of a camp for children with special needs, and later I'd worked as a special-needs tutor for many years. During my rabbinical school training, I was blessed with an opportunity to lead regular prayer services for families and children with special needs. So Anne's story hit home for me. For me, inclusion isn't a "nice to have" bonus or window-dressing for communities of faith; it's an ethical imperative. Without it, I wasn't sure we could call ourselves a house of God.

Anne's story inspired me to action. We spent the next year holding house meetings, expanding our network of families and children with special needs, and listening to their stories of hope and heartbreak. Once we had a sizable group, I proposed that we create a monthly prayer community designed specifically for the needs of this group. I used the tunes and liturgy that I had learned from my prayer leadership experience and worked with several families to decorate our chapel with bright colors, provide comfortable seating, and offer a number of accommodations to make it accessible and welcoming.

The first gathering was phenomenal—warm and loving. It felt like the kind of place where families painfully conscious of their differences could finally feel at home. And each month's gathering got progressively better. More families found their way to us, and more participants felt at home in our chapel. By our sixth service, a generous donor stepped forward to ensure that the service could run in perpetuity, under my leadership.

There was one problem. By the time this fledgling little community hit its stride, I had already decided to move on from my role at the synagogue to take a national-level position at my current organization, Clal - The National Jewish Center for Learning and Leadership.[3] I scrambled in my last few months at the synagogue to train new leaders for the monthly services. I encouraged the community to keep going without me. But it was too late. While my heart had been in the right place—I wanted nothing more than to serve these families as best I could—I had failed to give them what they needed most from me: encouragement and support to lead the community on their own.

Within six months of my departure from the synagogue, the community shifted from services to potlucks, and soon after from potlucks to nothing at all. The distinctive all-are-welcome-and-we-mean-it message of that synagogue felt less emphatic. A whole lot of families with differently abled children lost the place that, ever so briefly, had felt like their oasis. What that community had needed from me wasn't just my ability to lead services; it was an invitation for them to hold the power of gathering for themselves. I had failed them.

Almost a decade later, this failure has stayed with me. Each week, I roam the halls of the same synagogue on Shabbat morning with my family, and while I enjoy watching what the synagogue is becoming under new and visionary leadership, I can still hear the raucous rounds of "Thank you, God!" I remember from that brief time. I'm heartened by the memory of something that was so special while it lasted, and I'm haunted by its absence. So these days, in each of my roles—they range from father to supervisor to rabbi—I try my best to live up to the "iron rule" that my former supervisor, Sister Maribeth Larkin,[4] taught me on my first day as a community organizer: never do for others what they can learn to do for themselves. And while the lesson was a painful one to learn, I'm blessed each day to witness my children, my colleagues, and my students all learning to live into their gifts in ways they wouldn't be able to if not for this revelation.

Falling into Change: Kathi's Story

For more than thirty years, my work included responsibility for leading people, as a manager, a pastor, a senior administrator, a chair of one thing or another. I gravitate toward leadership; sometimes it's hard for me to sit quietly as part of a group being led by someone else. For a long time, I thought of leadership as my particular calling from God. That word seemed to hold the breadth of my positions and inclinations. It was a current that led me in and out of jobs and volunteer roles in churches, academic institutions, and other organizations.

So after three decades in leadership roles, I was pretty good at it, at least by some measures. I climbed the ladders that each position set before me. I led progressively larger churches; people seemed to welcome my thoughts and time. I got more skilled at thinking strategically, articulating a vision, and not overreacting to either criticism or compliments. I learned from my mistakes; I could at least recognize the times when I was moving so fast that I inadvertently rolled right over someone. Sometimes I could even stop myself from doing it.

About halfway through my career in ministry, I stumbled into a major professional setback. I held a senior leadership position in a seminary, a well-established theological school that was several years into a long-term decline in enrollment and financial health. I was asked to direct a commission that would study and make recommendations about the possibility of a new, more viable strategic direction for the institution. For two years, as the seminary's regular work continued, the commission explored innovations that might steer this 150-year-old institution toward a reframing of its mission, a transformation that would accommodate the needs of new kinds of students and the changing climate of faith-based social change. This was the most wide-open, exciting, possibility-laden work I had ever done. We closed the commission's work with a proposal that we believed was both excitingly radical and deeply grounded in the school's history and culture.

For months, I tentatively shared the vision with conversation partners around the country; they too thought our proposal was interesting, fresh, well-reasoned. The seminary's board of trustees was initially intrigued. They supported investing more of the school's resources in this direction. But the faculty? Not so much. Our proposal, they argued, would require too much change, too fast. It didn't adequately take into account the people whose jobs would be affected. It discarded—dishonored, in their view—many of the institution's long traditions. What followed was a long and messy conflict. The faculty would not move from their resistance. The board retreated. The project was terminated. I left my position.

I was naively shocked by the tactics I watched the plan's opponents use to drive home their points. I was angry at the people who gave up support for the proposal so quickly. I felt unseen, unappreciated, unfairly treated. As we do.

For a long time afterward—years—I felt the sting of that failure, acutely. I nursed my anger and soreness. It took me a few years, and the distance created by time and other opportunities for good work, to see the ways that I too had contributed to this painful chapter not only in my life but in the seminary's. I began to see that I and others had not managed the change process skillfully. We unwisely opted for rolling out a full vision all at once at the end of the process, expecting others to be as excited about it as we were. We hadn't provided enough opportunities for the faculty to engage in the process along the way. We didn't ask enough questions or listen carefully enough to the answers.

I know now that the breakdown came because of a failure of leadership—mine and others'. There are many things we—I—could have done differently. It was a deeply humiliating moment in my professional life; there is no other way to say it. But the world is more forgiving than we sometimes expect it to be. I have had other chances to lead. I have not made exactly the same mistakes again.

After I left the seminary, I returned to leading congregations, where resistance to change is no less present, but it is usually less organized. I carried with me the humbling lessons of a failed experiment. Those lessons became the platform from which a new experiment began: regarding every person—staff, laypeople, external partners—as partners with ideas and insights and opinions as valuable as my own. I listened more and talked less (I think). I shifted my focus from the smart, capable exercise of my power to empowering other people to lead alongside, sometimes instead of, me. That shift changed everything. And it led to the most fruitful years of my professional life.

The path of leadership for me has not been an enlightened ascension. It has certainly not felt glorious. Once again, years later, as I recently closed my career of leading churches, I felt a familiar consciousness of my weaknesses. I'd imagined that as I retired, I would gracefully, beneficently, hand off responsibility for my church to a next generation of leaders who would be profoundly grateful for the wisdom I'd accumulated and put to work. Ha! As it turned out, I spent my last year of active ministry feeling as uncertain that I'd mastered my leadership calling as I ever have.

The Way Up Is the Way Down

Occasions of unnerving self-doubt are essential stops on the path to conscious, non-ego-driven leadership. The writer and contemporary theologian Andy Crouch encourages regular sabbaticals, for their ability to drive leaders toward that digression. "The sabbatical year is . . . a discipline that tames power," he writes. "Sabbaticals force us to relinquish our sense of indispensability. So they subvert the god-playing that can afflict [us]. The truth is that others are fully able to fill the roles we set aside."[5] Without at least occasional reminders of our own *in*-capacity, we're likely to think we're helping when in fact we're straining the substance out of others' contributions to our common work.

In *The Power of Giving Away Power*, Matthew Barzun retells a story from the life of the legendary fundraiser Lynne Twist. Out of her own sense of calling to altruistic work, Twist made a four-day trek to meet with a leader of the Achuar people in the Amazon rainforest. Through an interpreter, she explained to the tribal leader why she was there. "The chief listened carefully and then said, 'I think I understand.' He considered his response for a moment. 'If you are here to help, please leave.' Oh no, she thought. That didn't go well. But then he continued, 'But if you are here because you feel your liberation is bound up with ours, then stay—let's work together.'"[6] Humiliation is sometimes the bearer of a necessary humility.

The Covid pandemic forced many of us toward a startling confrontation with the edges of our confidence. Even before the pandemic, the techniques of successful leadership of religious organizations seemed fragile, only unpredictably effective. Two-plus years of interruption in the patterns of the organizations undid much of what we thought we knew about how to lead successfully. The slow walk back to normal required religious leaders—everyone, really—to face a changed world. Regular volunteers and participants took the opportunity, sometimes with only slightly masked relief, to develop new routines. It was easier after that long intermission for them to say no to the commitments they used to feel responsible for. Staff members seemed to feel free to choose actions that were good for them but not the organization. Leaders were left even more alone, feeling more responsible for the whole enterprise than ever before.

Every thoughtful leader knows this moment of self-doubt—the sudden realization that everything you have, every ounce of energy and commitment you have been willing to pour out, might not be enough to hold a triumphant story together or to carry your people into their ultimate calling. The sneaking suspicion that it's not just their recalcitrance that freezes the organization in place, resistant to a larger vision and unable to move forward. It's you.

Adaptive leadership theory teaches that in every organization, the instant when leadership sparks resistance—when the link between the leader and followers threatens to snap—is a moment to learn from, an invaluable data point.[7] "Everything has a crack in it; that's how the light gets in," are the wise, weary words of the poet Leonard Cohen.[8] "I have prayed for years for one good humiliation a day," writes the Franciscan theologian Richard Rohr.[9] Painful as they are, moments of honest inadequacy are necessary turning points for every leader.

Those moments when our failures (or our fear of them) come into sharp focus also hold our epiphanies. Perhaps you feel like you are teetering on the dangerous edge of the foundation that used to underpin your leadership. That solid thing you were standing on has slipped a little; maybe you have, too. You could fall.

You are exactly where you need to be.

▲

Coming Unglued:
Moses's Story

Moses and God have a special, unbreakable connection. Moses takes his role seriously. He knows—everyone knows—that it is Moses's singular relationship with God that has brought them their freedom. This is what it means to be the leader: to hold for the entire tribe of Israelites their relationship with the Holy. To understand what they can't, to listen for the Voice, the answers, in a way they surely could never hear for themselves.

All their actions acknowledge and reinforce the pyramid shape of this congregation. From the beginning, Moses occupies a singular space at the top of a pyramid that arranges others into their places. The people do not resist, or even question, Moses's leadership. In fact, they depend on this arrangement. It lends them clarity not only about Moses's authority but also about their own responsibility. What is expected of them will be made clear from above; they rely on their leader to make sure everything else is managed. It's comforting, actually. The positions assigned to them stake out the boundaries of their actions. Not so different from what they were accustomed to as slaves in Egypt. When they are hungry, they complain to Moses, and he delivers the miracle of manna. When they are afraid, it is Moses's job to reassure them. When they have conflicts among themselves, Moses judges who is right and who is wrong.

When the Israelites arrive at the foot of Mount Sinai, the Exodus writers say, *they entered the wilderness of Sinai and encamped in the wilderness. Israel encamped there in front of the mountain, and Moses went up to God. God called to him from the mountain, saying, "Thus shall you say to the house of Jacob and declare to the children of Israel: 'You have seen what I did to the Egyptians, how I bore you on eagles' wings and brought you to Me. Now then, if you will obey Me faithfully and keep My covenant, you shall be My treasured possession among all the peoples. Indeed, all the earth is Mine, but you shall be to Me a kingdom of priests and a holy nation.' These are the words that you shall speak to the children of Israel." (Exod 19:2-7)*

Moses embraces the authority of his role, his speaking for God. If he has become an idol of sorts, a physical receptacle for the people's imagination of hope, well, then perhaps it is necessary for the arduous, unmapped journey before them. "Moses came and summoned the elders of the people and put before them all that God had commanded him. All those assembled answered as one, saying, 'All that God has spoken we will do!'" (Exod 19:8). Automatically, the people agree to what they are told. Everything that the Lord has said we will do. Of course they say this; it's the right answer.

But God is a distant third party to this conversation; it's Moses they address. The words of God come in Moses's voice. The people speak to Moses, not to God. The loyalty, the mutual fidelity, embodied in this covenant is hazy. Their own connection to the divine is vague. They make the vow Moses asks of them, but they have only a faint understanding of what they are agreeing to. Their position at the base of the pyramid is a long way from its apex, and their promises are equally distant. They are responding to a voice only Moses can hear. The connection is thin.

They arrive at Mount Sinai, far enough from Egypt to imagine there might be another place that will be home, detached long enough from their slave bindings to know themselves as choice-bearing creatures. The God who has led them this far has proved worthy of their trust. Moses goes up the mountain to meet God, to seek the terms of the covenant that will spell out the terms of a less conditional relationship. For forty days he basks in spiritual retreat, time alone with God. They talk together; they deepen their bond. Maybe they strategize a little about the future. At the end of the retreat, God will summarize with a single finger. God will write their resolutions on tablets of stone. The time goes fast for Moses, as it does when you are absorbed in something, someone, you love.

Down below, forty days feels like an eternity. For almost six weeks, the people stand around at the foot of the mountain, waiting for their leader to come back. Moses's absence begins to feel less like a mission, more like abandonment. There is no one else who can tell them what to do; no one else who can assuage their anxiety or articulate—again—their purpose. The truth of their powerlessness is suddenly evident, and it is uncomfortable. And so the people fill in the empty space with anxious worry. Is Moses gone forever? Have they been left out here on their own? Who named Moses king, anyway?[10]

It is not God they doubt; God was never within reach. It's Moses they begin to mistrust because it's Moses they had come to revere and to depend on. Moses's overfunctioning as a leader corresponds with—and perhaps has encouraged—a commensurate frailty in the people. The more he took on, the less capable they became.

They crave compulsively a commanding, always-present leader. Someone they can see and touch, someone who will answer questions and speak to their fears. Someone who will meet their uncertainty with masterful reassurance in this out-in-the-wilderness campground. With Moses, they can ignore their discomfort with a God who eludes their grasp and confounds them again and again. Without Moses, they are unsettlingly close to the truth of their lostness.

Aaron, Moses's second-in-command, sees the increasing impatience, the restlessness, of the people. He doesn't try to fill the leadership vacuum himself—he knows he cannot take Moses's place—but he can temporarily relieve the people's anxiety. He gives them something to do.

> Aaron said to them, "[You men,] take off the gold rings that are on the ears of your wives, your sons, and your daughters, and bring them to me." And all the people took off the gold rings that were in their ears and brought them to Aaron. This he took from them and cast in a mold, and made it into a molten calf. And they exclaimed, "This is your god, O Israel, who brought you out of the land of Egypt!" (Exod 32:2–4)

Traditional biblical interpretation frequently pairs Aaron with the people's sin, as though the golden calf illustrates his disobedience, and his loss of faith. The midrash is more nuanced. Perhaps, the midrash suggests, Aaron knows that the people needed something stabilizing in that moment, a call to the practices of piety. Perhaps he senses that the people have overinvested their trust in Moses.[11]

Andy Crouch writes, "Idolatry is the biblical name for the human capacity for creative power to run amok."[12] The calf was a classic god figure in the place they came from; its statue is a familiar sight. However misguided, the golden calf is Aaron's material rendering of a truth no one has yet articulated: even on the other side of the Red Sea, the Israelites still sleep in the shadow of the great pyramids. Generations of life in Egypt have formed the shape of their world and informed their place in it. A calf ingeniously fashioned from the gold the people carried out of slavery was an expressive, curious articulation of the people's power, and of their powerlessness.

Aaron's creation—an inanimate, speechless idol made out of precious metals removed from the people's ears and wrists—is the perfect representation, a mimicking of what they need and expect of their leader: predictability, steadiness. This leader will ask them for the obedience of their bodies but not the strength of their convictions. And in exchange, an idolized leader will protect them from seeing the vastness of the empty desert all around them, the expansiveness that triggers a toxic mix of anxiety about the road ahead and nostalgia for the one behind.

Moses's delay in returning from the mountain is taken as evidence that he has abandoned the obligations of leadership that life in the empire has taught the people to depend on. This moment is the one that demonstrates, above all others, that the people are not yet free. They are still slaves, impatiently waiting for their master to return. They have simply transferred their obedience from Pharaoh to Moses.

From this moment on, *stiff-necked* is how the Israelites will be described, by Moses and even by God. Stubborn, unfaithful, difficult to lead. But what the Israelites demonstrate in the golden-calf incident is not infidelity; it's overattachment to their leader. It's Moses's direction they miss and that they are lost without. Their ears are not attuned to the unfamiliar sound of divine counsel. They have not yet discovered that God's voice can resonate in them, too, and that Moses's mediation will not substitute for their wholehearted response. Like Moses's, the people's place in the pyramid is fixed, immovable. Their animation, their genuine responsiveness, will come only with their empowerment, the existential and spiritual freedom that will eventually accompany their physical liberation.

If Moses is gone, they simply transfer their praise from Moses's God to another object. The people genuflect before an altar on which the golden calf is theatrically placed. They eat, drink, and dance. It's a festival!

At the top of the mountain, God can see the insurrection going on below. "Hurry down!" God says to Moses, "for your people, whom you brought out of the land of Egypt, have acted basely" (Exod 32:7). At first, Moses is unperturbed. He knows his people. He can't see what God sees, but whatever mischief they've gotten into, he is confident he can handle it.

God is less sanguine. Whatever it is that's going on down there, this time the people have crossed a line, apparently. God's anger burns hot, hotter than Moses has felt it before. In God's mouth, they're no longer "my people"; they're "your" people, even "this" people (Exod 32:9).[13] The moderating voice is Moses's. He pleads with God on their behalf; he implores God to give them another chance. He uses clever, lawyerly arguments. Don't give the Egyptians rhetorical ammunition against you, Moses cajoles. "Let not the Egyptians say, 'It was with evil intent that he delivered them, only to kill them off in the mountains and annihilate them from the face of the earth'" (Exod 32:12).[14]

And remarkably—not for the first time or the last, but always notably—God relents. In an act of inordinate grace, God agrees to refrain from destroying the rebellious tribe below. God sends Moses back down the mountain, still carrying the stone tablets on which God has etched, with God's own finger, the commandments of mutual covenant, the commandments whose writing seems almost synchronized with the people's turn toward a figurine. The commandments that Moses has, for the moment, convinced God not to revoke.

It isn't until Moses approaches the camp and hears the music that he begins to get angry. The rabbis say that it was the people's dancing that threw him into a rage.[15] Until that moment, his confidence in the clarity of his position was complete. These were his people. He had staked his relationship with God on his sureness that he could readily redirect them, press them back into line. As soon as they saw him, he guessed, the moment they recognized his shape coming down the mountain, the people would remember the promise of obedience they had just made to their God. To Moses's God.

Would the music stop when someone noticed Moses approaching the camp? Would the dancing cease? Would they stare down at their feet self-consciously or throw a towel over the offending statue? Any one of those signs of conscience might have aroused Moses's sympathy, tempered his anger, regathered the tether between him and the Israelites. But none of these things happen. They keep dancing, circling their metal idol shamelessly. As if Moses's faith—the genuine leaning of his soul toward the God who saw the Israelites' oppression and offered freedom instead, the God who engineered an escape route from their slave quarters and through the Red Sea, the God who stood watch for them in pillars of fire and cloud—is not their faith at all.

Something true comes into focus, startlingly. Moses's dependence on God's leading has not been mirrored by the Israelites. He has assumed it, erroneously. The hope that Moses drew from his interactions with God, the people have been seeking elsewhere: in Moses himself. Moses had wanted to believe that the words he had heard God speak had been imprinted on their hearts too. But he was wrong.

He has felt it before, this separation of leader from the rest, the weight of his singular responsibility. He has been frustrated before, in moments when he saw a vision they could not yet discern. But now, something tangible has broken. In actions far more potent than words, the people have demonstrated that while their bodies may have followed him into the wilderness, their hearts did not. When he fails their expectations, they simply turn in another direction. Inside him, something fractures. A piece or two falls away. The tiny space he has occupied at the apex of the pyramid has detached from the rest of the structure. Moses is inconsolable. He is isolated. And for the first time, Moses is truly alone.

Notes

1 Credit to the Japanese proverb *Nana korobi, ya oki* (Fall down seven times, stand up eight).

2 A *kippah* is a traditional Jewish head covering meant to convey a sense of humility before God.

3 Elan's first role at Clal - The National Jewish Center for Learning and Leadership was director of innovation. He now serves as its executive vice president.

4 A Sister of Social Service, Sister Maribeth Larkin was Elan's supervisor and mentor during his time as a community organizer with OneLA, an affiliate with the Industrial Areas Foundation network (https://www.onela-iaf.org/).

5 Crouch, *Playing God*, 260.

6 Barzun, *Power of Giving Away Power*, 97–98.

7 Heifetz, Linsk, and Grashow, *Practice of Adaptive Leadership*.

8 Leonard Cohen, "Anthem," track number five on *The Future*, Columbia, 1992.

9 Richard Rohr, *Falling Upward: A Spirituality for the Two Halves of Life* (San Francisco: Jossey-Bass, 2011), 128.

10 "As for *this man Moses* who brought us up out of the land of Egypt, we don't have a clue what has happened to him" (Exod 32:1, paraphrased in Avivah Zornberg, *The Particulars of Rapture* [New York: Schocken Books, 2001], 400).

11 Zornberg, *Particulars of Rapture*, 402–4.

12 Crouch, *Playing God*, 55.

13 Notice parallel to Exod 39:2—the people's reference to "this man Moses"—when they lose their patience waiting for him.

14 Already Moses has distinguished himself as a leader. Notice the contrast with Noah's passively self-serving response to the divine offer to save him and his family from harm while the rest of humanity is destroyed by a flood.

15 Zornberg, *Particulars of Rapture*, 420–21.

Interlogue: Shattered

In so far as they represented everything shattered,
everything lost, they were the law of broken things,
the leaf torn from the stem in a storm, a cheek touched
in fondness once but now the name forgotten.
How they must have rumbled, clattered on the way
even carried so carefully through the waste land,
how they must have rattled around until the pieces
broke into pieces, the edges softened
crumbling, dust collected at the bottom of the ark
ghosts of old letters, old laws. In so far
as a law broken is still remembered
these laws were obeyed.

—Rodger Kamenetz, "The Broken Tablets"

Broken into Pieces

As soon as Moses takes in the scene of his people dancing ecstatically around the altar, on which a golden calf sits alone, this figurine of faithlessness, he reacts instinctually. He uses the only instruments he has in his hands: the blocks of stone he has carried with him down the mountain. With furious strength, he lifts the stones above his shoulders and casts them to the ground, hard. They smash into pieces, shatter into bits of words, spliced sentences. The sound of the crash—stone on stone—stops the music cold. The people stand in stunned silence while the shards of holy words scatter and find their place on the hardened dirt.

The midrash imagines that at Moses's sight of the idolatrous dancing, the letters flew away into the air. The effervescence of the relationship contained in the covenantal words evaporated, leaving the full weight of the stone tablets behind. Moses simply could not hold them any longer.[1] Was it heaviness that made them drop, or was it the rush of anger that raised the stones over Moses's head and hurled them? No matter. They are now in pieces. For Moses and for the people both, something fundamental has broken.

Many of us have known this moment—or fear for this moment—in our leadership. Things turn. Some of us think we have made a big mistake, or we know we have. Our confidence ebbs so far that we become convinced it will never flow again. Others' mistrust of us feels irrevocable. The fight-or-flight operation of the amygdala slips into gear inside of us, as it no doubt does for Moses. He must be thinking about just walking away, separating himself from these people who deserved to wander around in the wilderness unaided. He wonders, unsure, whether God's offer to wipe them out and start over with a new promise, to a new people, is still on the table. An immense self-discipline is necessary to calm himself and to call the people to order again.

Sifting through the Rubble

Here we see the first inkling of Moses's relinquishment of the leader's self-possessed command. For the first time, he stands not at their head but among them. He asks, "Who is on the Lord's side?" The decision required now is not a referendum on Moses's leadership; this is about their willingness to commit themselves to a God who will always be elusive, who will make no promise to never disappear again. A God who is capable of anger, who does not sit quietly on an altar of the people's construction. A God who will make demands of them, expect of them an engagement of their own. They must decide for themselves, just as Moses once decided for himself. This might be the first time they have been asked.

Not all of them move toward this God. Many choose something different. Three thousand people are lost that day, the text notes (Exod 32:28).[2] Imagine the elevator fall Moses must feel in his stomach as he watches his people self-organize, some choosing to stay with the project that is the work of his life, some stepping away as though it means nothing. Would it have made a difference if he had been more inspiring from the beginning? What if he had not reacted so emotionally when he came down the mountain and saw them dancing?

But Moses does not try to talk them into staying. He does not cover for them or make concessions that would make the rest of this journey less tense, more effortless. He acts, perhaps for the first time, like the "differentiated leader" that this golden-calf incident has startled him into becoming.[3] He watches as the people respond to the stirrings of their own hearts—not his. He watches as some choose what he would not choose for them.

There is a poignant moment in the story that happens here: "The next day Moses said to the people, 'You have been guilty of a great sin. Yet I will now go up to God; perhaps I may win forgiveness for your sin.' Moses went back to God and said, 'Alas, this people is guilty of a great sin in making for themselves a god of gold. Now, if You will forgive their sin [well and good]; but if not, erase me from the record which You have written!'" (Exod 32:30–32).

Curiously, Moses feels the need to bargain again with God on behalf of the inconstant Israelites. Why? God has already spoken words of restraint. God agreed, even before Moses came down the mountain, to forebear from punishing them. But then, Moses had not known the degree of the people's defection. He had not yet seen for himself the ecstasy on their faces as they danced around an altar with an artificial deity as its centerpiece. Now he comprehends the extent of their wrongdoing.

Is Moses's renewed appeal to God an effort to reconcile on their behalf, or is it for himself, too? Now Moses has joined them in their sin. The memory of his own anger, the reflex reaction that broke into smithereens the only writing that had ever emanated from the very finger of God, weighs heavily on Moses. *His* loss of control had erased the one remaining inscription of the people's connection with the Holy.

In the fragments of stone lying at his feet, Moses sees brokenness in the whole enterprise. We can imagine the cascade of defeats that must have run through his mind. Every leader knows them. *This project was ill-conceived from the beginning. I was never going to be able to lead these people. They never trusted me. It's their fault. It's my fault. No, it's their fault.*

Moses's isolation, his defeat, eclipses everything else; he has a 360-degree view of failure. But even in his bruised state, Moses gathers up enough courage to approach God one more time. He dares to propose forgiveness: not just a standoff, but full restoration of the people's favor with the God they have collectively betrayed. In a foreshadowing of what Christians will recognize as Jesus's atoning self-sacrifice, Moses offers himself as the agent of relationship repair. He raises the stakes. Their sin is his sin; their ending will be his ending, too. Please forgive their sin, he implores, "but if not, erase me from the record which You have written!'" (Exod 32:32). If they are lost, then he is lost, too.

That's How the Light Gets In

When God summons him to receive the second set of commandments, Moses trudges up the side of Mount Sinai carrying the weight of both the people's sin and his own. Now he knows: he is no different from the people he leads. He does not stand apart. It is a chastened Moses who climbs Mount Sinai again. Like the stone tablets, like the pyramid-shaped structure of their life together, he's broken too. He had thought that if he kept climbing to a higher elevation, he and God could huddle together until he was so full of God's vision, he could carry it back down the mountain in his own body. He had tried to make himself a rough stand-in for the God he didn't trust the people to see for themselves. He thought he could, with discipline, work ethic, and faith, bridge the gap between an elusive holiness and a very human discomfort with uncertainty. But no, he sees now that he, their leader, was incapable of bearing such a burden. The power that had been entrusted to him lies broken at his feet.

Perhaps this is what the desert wilderness experience is for: to bring us to moments of nakedness before God that Moses now knows. The theologian and scholar Belden Lane writes of moments like this,

> This is T. S. Eliot's "wasteland," where language breaks down and relationships shatter—a desert so utterly threatening, and yet familiar, to modern consciousness. It is a bitter end, but it offers a new beginning. We cannot imagine letting go of the mastery of reality that our words once occasioned for us; and yet we know our words to be hollow . . . realizing that our only way out of the desert is to go deeper into it . . . to the "still point" where God meets us in emptiness.[4]

Even here, even now, the hopefulness of God, the capacity to forgive, is apparently inexhaustible. Not even the wildly unrighteous golden-calf worshipers are wiped out of God's scroll. Nor is Moses, his unrestrained anger on full display. The commandments are reinscribed, on an intact set of stone tablets. By the grace of God, the covenant survives.

This is the moment of turning for Moses. It is not so dramatic as a rethinking of God's covenant with the people of

Israel. It's not even a reconsideration of his own essential faith. But like the recovering alcoholic's hitting bottom or the prodigal son's coming to himself, this is the moment when Moses surrenders. He knows that something must change, that *he* must change. It is not God's grace that is in question; it's the contours of Moses's ego, his understanding of what it means to be called a leader of this people.

The Story's Postscript

The Exodus text suggests a tender tentativeness in the relationships all around following the golden-calf incident. Moses withdraws a little while; he reimagines his place among the people. He pitches his tent outside the campsite. He veils himself when he walks among them, perhaps as a gesture of self-protection, or perhaps self-restraint. When he goes into the tent to speak with God, the people watch from a distance; they see him only from the back, just as Moses will be invited to see only God's back in the cleft between boulders (Exod 33:23). It will take a little while for the bruises to heal and for the congregation to take a new shape. As they pack up camp and resume their journey through the wilderness, as God renews the promise to lead this people of questionable faith into the land that has been promised, each is a little more tender than before. Their steps forward are a little more tentative.

There are two more stories in the biblical and midrashic texts that signal the powerful residue of this incident. "When the people heard this harsh word, they went into mourning, and none put on finery. God said to Moses, 'Say to the Israelite people, "You are a stiff-necked people. If I were to go in your midst for one moment, I would destroy you. Now, then, leave off your finery, and I will consider what to do to you."' So the Israelites remained stripped of their finery from Mount Horeb on" (Exod 33:4–6).

On that first Passover night when they left all the rest of their possessions behind, a few rings, earrings, and bracelets were all they could carry with them, a meager remnant of the security that life in the empire had offered. Now they remove it all—the people and Moses both. Their jewelry, fancier clothing, perhaps their more colorful fabrics, the last remnants of value they carried with them from life in Egypt. They are stripped of the accessories that have continued to link them to life in the shadow of the pyramids. Perhaps now they can be free.

The second set of tablets, bearing the repeated commandments from God, will be handled like the evidence of second chances, the holy treasure they are. Later, they will be displayed in the temple's space known as the holy of holies. For now, they are placed in the ark of the covenant. When the company moves along in their journey toward the promised land, the ark will be carried ahead of them, the symbol of God's continuing presence, the object of their ritual devotion, their meticulous care.

There is a midrashic tradition that places inside the ark, together with the second set of stones, the fragments of the original, broken tablets. Shattered, illegible traces of words and promises, picked up piece by piece from the ground, swept painstakingly into a pile, placed carefully into the holy container. These, too—debris from the moment when everything broke apart—will be carried into the promised land. This memory, too, belongs in the story of their becoming the people of God.[5]

Perhaps the evidence of brokenness, both Moses's and his people's, was the only thing that could reveal to Moses a truth he could not see before. Leadership of God's people would not mirror the image of the Egyptian pharaoh Moses grew up watching. The congregation that would reach the promised land would not be shaped like the empire that enslaved them.

Like every moment that yields transformation, Moses's memory of the grotesque scene where he stood among the shattered words of God becomes his pivot point—the "until one day" of his transformation story. It was an ending that might have been absolute. His crisis of faith, of confidence, of relationship turns him toward the countenance of a God for whom obedience is only a step on the way to love. A God who had imagined a different, fuller freedom for people and leader alike.

There in the shadow of Mount Sinai, bent before the shattered pieces of holy stones, Moses is released from the image of the unquestionable, self-sufficient leader he thought he had to be.

The rabbi and Jewish scholar Lawrence Kushner writes: "The memories of a place become a part of it. Places and things never forget what they have been witnesses to and vehicles of and entrances for. What has happened there happened nowhere else. Like ghosts who can neither forget what they have seen nor leave the place where they saw it, such are the memories tied to places of ascent."[6]

And, we might add, such are the memories tied to places of descent, too. The ascent of a true leader is never unbroken. Only when Moses climbs Mount Sinai again, carrying the full weight of the people's rebellion and consciousness of his own incompleteness, does the pyramid Moses had carried in his body, all the way from Egypt, crumble. As it must. A pyramid is not a shape that will contain the character of God. And it cannot confine the life of a people who were made to be free.

Notes

1 Zornberg, *Particulars of Rapture*, 423–24.
2 Depending on your theology and exegetical philosophy, you may read the text about Moses's instruction to kill three thousand Israelites in a variety of ways. Surely the text reflects a human tendency to project our instincts toward retribution onto God. Did a civil war

erupt at that moment between those who wanted to follow the God of Abraham and those who wanted to rebuild the altar to the golden calf? Was it a plague that swept through the encampment? Did some of the Israelites simply leave the company and become "lost" to the followers of the Hebrew God?

3 This is Edwin Friedman's term for a leader who remains connected to a group while remaining unentangled by its anxiety (*Failure of Nerve*).

4 Belden C. Lane, *The Solace of Fierce Landscapes* (Oxford: Oxford University Press, 2007), 67.

5 Zornberg, *Particulars of Rapture*, 456; b. Menahot 99a.

6 Lawrence Kushner, *Honey from the Rock: Ten Gates of Jewish Mysticism* (Woodstock, VT: Jewish Lights, 1999), 54.

Part II

Distancing from the Empire That Shaped Us

CHAPTER FIVE

What We Leave Behind

Lessons from a Pizza Parlor: Kathi's Story

I'd been sent by a retreat leadership team to pick up pizzas for early-arriving participants. When I arrived, I was told something had gone awry with the order, so I had about fifteen minutes in an almost empty restaurant (late-stage pandemic era) to stand in front of the counter and watch the operations as about eight employees tried to make up some time as the restaurant began to fill on this Friday night.

I watched as each person snapped into their spot to play their role in the open kitchen. One lifted the ball of dough and stretched it flat; the next eyed the order, then slathered on the right toppings. Two stood at an open wood-fire oven, holding spatulas with broom handles, shuffling pizzas from front to back, side to side. Out the pizzas came—pretty quickly, it seemed to me—to be sliced and boxed by another guy, standing by for his cue.

In between all these folks, moving around with what looked to me like blistering speed, was the manager, a young guy who was clearly feeling great responsibility for the production underway. In the minutes while I stood there, he elbowed one employee after another out of the way so that he could do their job for them. He didn't say anything to them directly, but he huffed a lot in a way that quietly indicated his disapproval. He moved faster than they did. He sliced more fluidly. He deftly handled every ingredient with an economy of movement unparalleled by his peers. And just to make sure his colleagues

fully understood his severe disappointment in their performance, he dumped two perfectly good-looking pizzas that they
had made into the garbage, all without a word.

The crew got quieter; the banter between them stopped.
Every employee pressed to the periphery of the kitchen, out of
their manager's way. They stood there frozen, awkward, unsure
what to do with their hands. Not only had their workflow been
interrupted, but their very sense of purpose and of place had
been undermined.

This extraordinarily competent pizza-parlor manager might
have gotten a few pizzas out more efficiently than they would
have otherwise. But overall, it looked to me—even as he was the
one pushing them aside—that he was in the employees' way,
not the other way around.

He worked extraordinarily hard. I'm sure he thought he
was modeling productivity as he stepped into each position.
But what was most evident was the way he was intimidating
his staff—without once yelling like Gordon Ramsay or any of
the other celebrity chefs whose brand is built on bullying. His
wordless disappointment in them, visible in his compressed
lips and the sharp edges of his movements, was enough. I fully
expected one or two of the employees to quit at the end of their
shift.

I wonder how many times my leadership has looked like a
slightly more subtle version of what I saw that manager do in
the pizza restaurant that night. Sometimes consciously, sometimes not, I've behaved as though I thought being the one in
charge meant that I could do everyone else's job better than
they could. I've regularly run around trying to accomplish more
things faster, no doubt creating more dust than value. I know
I've left others feeling uncertain of what to do next, because I
hadn't taken the time to explain my brilliant new idea.

Leadership is hard for people who move fast. Leading
doesn't always require or reward the traits that made us prized

individual contributors. Expertise, valuable as it is, is better employed as a support, not a cudgel. If it's not exercised carefully, thoughtfully, and with ego restraint, it becomes an obstacle that others have to skirt before they can step into their own sense of ownership of their work.

Unlearned Lessons

There is, for us as it was for Moses, a necessary shattering, a moment when it becomes excruciatingly clear that the leader's vigilant protection of our defended position at the top is slowly crumbling the spirits of not only the people around us but our own spirits, too. Until that happens, the message floats hazily, visible but unexplained in the ambivalence of low-energy staff members, in volunteers who opt out, in the tepid response to initiatives launched with every ounce of energy and goodwill we can muster.

For Moses, there was no single "Aha!" moment after which new insight clicked into place. Neither did his shattering moment instantly propel him and the people he led into the land of milk and honey. Just like the painstaking process of gathering up the pieces of shattered tablets, Moses collected fragments of revelation throughout a long wilderness journey. Some made sense in the moment; others became his teachers only after he'd carried them in his pocket for years.

Like most significant changes in our lives, the most essential element in the transformation of our leadership is about unlearning things we have unconsciously internalized along the way. It's unnamed standards and unnoticed expectations that bear down on us most heavily. This is the invisible, inescapable power of culture; this is what consultants mean when they say, "Culture eats strategy for breakfast."[1] Hearing and learning new techniques, even setting different behavioral plans, is not enough. A different kind of leadership, intentional about sharing power rather than stockpiling it, cannot be layered on top of a set of contradictory practices and assumptions. There must be a process of disinheriting that goes first. Otherwise, we are just creating mental clutter.

Pixels and Pyramids: Rabbi Adam Kligfeld's Story

Wherever Rabbi Adam Kligfeld goes, he never travels alone; he is accompanied by words of Torah in all walks of his life. It came as no surprise, then, that a conversation about his leadership journey did not begin with a philosophy to which he subscribes, or even a personal story, but with a piece of Torah.

In a "Torah with Rashi" class that he had just finished with his congregants,[2] they were exploring a particularly heated exchange between Pharaoh and the overseers of the Israelites. Pharaoh has moved the goalposts on the slaves by forcing them to collect their own straw while still producing the same number of bricks as before, when the straw was provided for them.[3] The overseers advocate for the Israelites, imploring, "Why do you deal thus with your servants? No straw is issued to your servants, yet they demand of us: Make bricks! Thus your servants are being beaten, when the fault is with your own people" (Exod 5:15–16). Sensing the challenge that comes from their God, Pharaoh lashes out: "'You are shirkers, shirkers! That is why you say, 'Let us go and sacrifice to God.' Now, go and serve! No straw shall be issued to you, but you must produce your quota of bricks!" (Exod 5:17–18).

The wordplay that seems revelatory this morning concentrates on the word *ivdu*, which means to go and serve. The term refers both to the Israelites' status as slaves, *avadim*, and to their desire to serve their God through worship and sacrifice, *avodah*. Kligfled shares his own take on the implied comparison: "There's an *avdut* [enslavement] to Pharaoh, not at all the same as an *avdut* [service] to the *Kadosh Baruch Hu* [the Holy Blessed One]."[4]

It's that distinction between compulsory action and service that sits at the heart of Kligfeld's leadership ethos. From a very young age, he felt a connection to God. It took shape in both personal prayer and communal leadership; his earliest experiences as a leader came when he was elected to leadership in United Synagogue Youth, the youth group affiliated with the Conservative Movement of Judaism. Kligfeld says, "It may sound cliché, but back in USY when I was learning the notion of leadership, there was only one president. But each of the vice presidents had a lot of things to do, and the most important job of the president was not to do all of the work for them or gain all the glory, but to dissipate the *kavod* [honor]. That both made the job of the president easier and also made the people feel better about their work."[5]

Sharing the glory of leadership was not innate for Kligfeld. It was something he had to practice and internalize over time. "The seventeen-year-old version of myself had a less healthy relationship with ego than I do now," he says. "I was still learning that the other folks in the system needed and deserved spotlight and *kavod* [honor]. The system needed to contain that honor on their behalf."[6]

In that one comment, Kligfeld articulates the tension between working for Pharaoh and serving God, between climbing the levels of the pyramid to position yourself above others and journeying into the wilderness alongside them. He saw that tension in himself as he rose through the ranks of United Synagogue Youth, of Hillel while in college, and through each class of rabbinical school. This consciousness deepened his embrace of the generous leadership he now practices innately. The conversion from a seventeen-year-old, ego-driven youth leader to the rabbi who identifies his work as liberating others did not take place overnight. There were hard-won lessons along the way.

When Kligfeld first became a rabbi, he took a position at a small synagogue in Monroe, New York, located in the Hudson

Valley—a world apart from Manhattan's Morningside Heights neighborhood, where he had spent five years during rabbinical school. As far as he could tell, his agreement to serve as the congregation's rabbi would entail a variety of the tasks he'd been taught to anticipate: teaching, preaching, prayer leading, and officiating at life-cycle events for his new community. What he didn't realize was that in addition to those expected roles, he would also serve as administrative assistant, now-and-then maintenance person, senior executive, and just about every other role that came up. He remembers, "There was no pyramid in our organizational structure. It was a single pixel. I was the only professional. We had part-time Hebrew school teachers, and I had a fifteen-hour-a-week office manager. It was fanciful even to discuss the structure of the leadership of my *shul* [synagogue] in Monroe. It was me and any lay leaders I could get to do stuff."[7]

For ten years, Kligfeld was everywhere the community needed him to be. He built and nurtured close relationships with every single member of the community, from his students in the Hebrew school to decades-older members. He attended every meeting, from board events to routine committee meetings. He worked diligently before every prayer service to make sure they always had the ritually required ten people, whether it was a Wednesday morning in midwinter or Yom Kippur afternoon.

For rabbi and congregation both, it was a decade-long season of joy and gratitude. Kligfeld earned and enjoyed the trust of a tight-knit community; the *shul*'s membership and programming grew as their rabbi injected his trademark energy and depth into every aspect of its life. The Torah he always carried with him found its way into the minds and hearts of everyone around him. The congregation's confidence in him made room for experiences that nurtured and reinforced his skills as a pastoral leader. Kligfeld knew that the route many of his newly minted colleagues had taken out of rabbinical school (as assistant rabbis in large synagogues) would have yielded a fraction of his hands-on learning experience. What he gave up in pulpit size, he more than made up in a wealth of personal and spiritual growth.

When things are good, there's no reason to rock the boat. But when a prominent pulpit position opened up in Los Angeles, right in his in-laws' neighborhood, the position presented the perfect opportunity for Kligfeld's family and career. But this transition would demand more than just a cross-country move. The two synagogues were radically different. Monroe's synagogue was firmly entrenched in East Coast Conservative Judaism: more traditional, less inclined to embrace change. Los Angeles was the embodiment of the West Coast: cutting-edge and progressive. One building was small, intimate, and unassuming; the other campus sprawled across an entire block, with plans to expand further. One community was accustomed to a rabbi who did it all; the other had an elaborate leadership structure, with a myriad of lay-led committees and a large, capable staff.

Before he made his way west, Kligfeld prepared carefully to take on the different kind of leadership he knew would be required of him. He called other, more senior colleagues who had made similar moves in their careers and asked them for their wisdom and, from a few, for their mentorship. As he took close note of the experiences they shared, successes and failures alike, he heard guidance that was as much theological as it was practical. He heard in their advice an echo of the same lesson he had learned as a youth group leader decades before: *kavod* (glory) comes in many forms: power, honor, even anxiety. For the system to thrive, everyone needs to hold a share of that glory, in good times and bad times, too.

When Kligfeld arrived in his new role in Los Angeles, he discovered there were whole mindsets he'd needed to leave behind in Monroe. In his first ten years he had developed a leadership mode that suited the single-pixel structure of a small synagogue. In his old job, he'd felt solely responsible for ensuring the community's health and growth. Everything that happened at the synagogue had his fingerprints on it; every new movement was a product of his instinct, ideation, initiative. If he didn't dream it up and manifest it, it didn't happen. In his new role, that approach would quickly leave him burned out, his staff devalued, and his community disengaged: "In a small synagogue, the extent to which your vision is carried out is directly related to what you do. Everything that happens, you are doing. In a larger synagogue, the work is different. The senior rabbi's role is to nurture an effective board and build a professional team. So much of the work institutionally has to be done by them, not you."[8]

The proposition sounds obvious, but the practice is not. Like most clergy placed into positions of responsibility, Kligfeld was confident he was equipped to do the work required to run his new organization. He'd gone to school and earned an advanced degree in this exact field. He'd had ten years of experience with applying his classroom knowledge to real-world challenges. And he was wholeheartedly committed to serving this community. He was, without doubt, the most qualified, experienced, and well-positioned person in—or outside—the building. Certainly, he was the community member most invested in implementing the organization's vision. But that didn't mean he was the *right* person to do it on every occasion. Sometimes, he realized, if you are the only person carrying the ownership of a program or project, the best thing you can do for your community is to set that burden down, lovingly. If the folks around you come to miss whatever it was, then you have an opening to invite them into accountability and ownership, to empower them. And if they don't miss it, maybe it wasn't all that important to them in the first place.

Like many of us, Kligfeld had internalized the illusion that faster is always better. He'd learned to lead in a small, agile community. There, he'd been able to make changes with very little bureaucratic molasses slowing things down. In a larger system, making healthy change required gathering input from key stakeholders, holding to processes that prioritized clear communication, developing buy-in at multiple levels of the organization. All those steps require time and the discipline of a long patience.

> We want to change our rules about whether or not the girls in our community become bat mitzvah before age thirteen. I think that if we're egalitarian then we should no longer be relying on rabbinic texts that were focused on specific parts of maturing girls' physiologies,[9] but rather we should say adulthood is thirteen for both boys and girls. Well, I could just say it and make it happen and then deal with the fallout. Instead, we've invited the Ritual Committee to study this change together. I've asked all the female clergy to discuss it as well; I'm really invested in their feedback. I know that I am electing to disempower myself, which is going to slow down the process, but I hope it will lead us to a better outcome.[10]

Reflecting on this slow process, Kligfeld recognizes the tension between the urgency of the impulse toward change and an abiding faith that God's glory is not bound by deadlines and timelines. He feels the frustration that comes with the slow pace of communal deliberation.

> The longer you go in your life and your career, you realize how much less time you have coming up. I just turned fifty. That tells me how much active rabbinic leadership I have left. It's probably less than the active rabbinic leadership that I've had, which means tick, tick, tick, tick, tick. When time is ticking, you can get impatient, and you'd like to be a general, but that is a drawback. You have to have a willingness to be in the weeds with people.[11]

Once, as they worked together on a school research project, Kligfeld and his daughter Noa came upon a history of President Dwight Eisenhower's transition from military to presidential leadership. Eisenhower, they learned, struggled with the adjustment required of his leadership style. In the military, he could snap his fingers and an entire platoon would move on his command. But in his new post as president of the United States, getting things done wasn't so simple. He had to build a cabinet of advisers with knowledge in fields he could never master, wrestle with congressional leaders who drew their power by opposing his, and mobilize diverse coalitions. Kligfeld identified with Eisenhower's frustration. "Sometimes I'd like to operate by fiat," he says. "There are moments where I'd like to be a general. I know exactly how things should be done. But even if I could give myself that authority momentarily, I know it would break down in the long term."

Kligfeld's journey took him from a congregation on one coast of the country to one on the other, from a predictable, do-everything seat of leadership in a pixel-shaped congregation to a more nuanced role in a thriving, sprawling and deeply engaged community. As he has done throughout his life, he adapted along the way. He changed. He let go of the tools that no longer felt useful and sharpened new ones that did. Ironically, as he grew, he found that his new role was decidedly narrower than the previous one. He had to rely less on his own broad set of inherited and accumulated skills, more on the singular trait of Mosaic leaders: to invite others into full engagement in the organization's collective work. Now it is Kligfeld's own transformation that helps bring people alive—not by filling them with his inspiration and capability, but by leaving space for theirs.

Examining the Empire's Expectations

In a 2005 graduation speech at Kenyon College, the late writer David Foster Wallace opened with a parable: "There are these two young fish swimming along, and they happen to meet an older fish swimming the other way, who nods at them and says, 'Morning, boys. How's the water?' And the two young fish swim on for a bit, and then eventually one of them looks over at the other and goes, 'What the hell is water?'"[12]

Like those fish, we did not choose the cultural water in which we swim. Most of the time we're not even aware of it. The culture of empire is pervasive. Religious and secular leaders alike have inherited our cultural expectations of successful leadership, along with the assumptions that underlie those expectations. But those expectations and assumptions have gone unexamined for too long. Consider some of the ideals we have internalized about what makes for a good leader:

- **Good leaders have answers.** They calm their people's discomfort through their wisdom and sense-making capacities.
- **Good leaders are decisive.** The most successful leaders move fast, which allows their organizations to move fast, too.
- **Good leaders have natural charisma.** They shape the future by sheer force of personality.
- **Good leaders have most of the good ideas.** They take singular responsibility for the vision and strategy of the organization, and when there is dissonance among the ranks, leaders work to either quiet or convince those who question them.
- **Good leaders do not exhibit vulnerability.** On the rare occasions when they do, they carefully calculate the impression they convey to others.
- **Good leaders are always in control.** Their personal standards are visible everywhere—in what is produced by those who work "below" them and in organizational outcomes.

Individually, these assumptions seem effective, even responsible. But they fold into an unsustainable and often harmful set of expectations for conscientious leadership. Digging deeper reveals the fearful beliefs that underscore them:

Certainty is sacred. When leaders—lay, staff, and clergy—express uncertainty, organizations are at risk of losing their way.

Faster is better. There is always something chasing us or eluding us. We save ourselves by moving, by outpacing it.[13]

Leaders are rare. The qualities required for leadership—creativity, intellectual prowess, initiative, strategic consciousness—are scarce.

Conflict is corrosive. Collective enterprise requires a group that is of one mind; dissent is dangerous.

Leaders and followers don't mix. The leader must remain, in some essential way, separate from the people being led. Unregulated demonstrations of vulnerability risk piercing that firewall.

Everything goes through the leader. No important organizational function should happen unless the leader at the very least gives express approval.

Like Foster Wallace's proverbial fish, we might be surprised to learn that we have been swimming in cultural waters that celebrate these commonly held standards of leadership. Unconsciously, we have adopted their underlying assumptions as unassailable. Perhaps, if the proverb didn't end with a punchline, those fish might have later come to realize that they could seek new water in which to swim. Perhaps, as our story continues, we might, too.

When we stop to reexamine these standards, we can see the consequences they impose, the costs we have been willing to bear. We might even find ourselves feeling freer than perhaps we knew: to consciously choose the assumptions we will carry with us and to leave behind the embellishments of leadership that no longer serve well. Yes, we are swimming in toxic waters. But no, we are not required to stay.

The Things to Leave Behind

A General's Mindset

While no one would suggest that military ranks belong in every setting, in many organizations we've settled for an only slightly softened order. In the nonprofit world, it's still the executive director to whom connections with key donors and board members are reserved, just one person with whom the full picture of the organization's landscape resides. In religious organizations, it's the senior pastor or senior rabbi whose mastery includes the only direct pipeline to God (let alone the key donors). A commanding mentality is difficult to shed, for good reasons. Generals are the officers we trust with strategy; they know how to move forward and defeat enemies.

The thing is, the work of religious and nonprofit communities is primarily *not* about mobilizing to defeat enemies, or conquering the market. In fact, the mindset of strategic warfare fights with the values that underlie most religious theologies and sensibilities. A leader who looks past people to lead the organization's charge with the single-minded efficiency of a four-star general usually sacrifices the well-being that accompanies a genuine collective of open hearts and minds. The victory is admirable, but it is short-lived.

The Need for Speed

The technology revolution has generated a culture that celebrates leaders who "move fast and break stuff."[14] We've grown accustomed to collateral damage; we are adept at justifying it as means to the worthy end. But the broken stuff that fast company leaders leave behind isn't only what we can witness in real time, visible to the naked eye. There's more hidden damage with longer repercussions to people and to the trust between them. Fractured relationships are not so easily repaired. When leaders rush a decision-making process, there is opportunity lost: to deepen connections, even through disagreement; to offer a sense of shared ownership of the end result. Your instincts about the better result might have been right all along. But there is a lingering value to leadership that is patient enough to allow space for the leadership of others to emerge, for more voices to be heard, for a wider group to feel counted.

The Business of Busyness

Many, if not most, leaders of religious organizations are overworked. We know that; numerous studies have documented the danger of clergy exhaustion and burnout.[15] Hypertension, obesity, and depression are common. But many leaders hold on to exhaustion as if it were a badge of honor. "So often we go about our duties as if they will save us," wrote a United Methodist pastor taking a first sabbatical in many years of ministry, even though the denomination's *Book of Discipline* had offered him one many times over. "I felt guilty at the thought of an extended break from my work-a-day duties. I was uneasy about continuing to draw my regular salary while I 'wasn't working.'"[16] Brené Brown calls this cultural idolatry: exhaustion as a status symbol, overfunctioning as a measure of self-worth.[17]

Perhaps we do this because there are so few metrics by which to assess the success of pastoral and other nonprofit leadership. When measurable outcomes of our work are hard to come by, leaders take stock of input, which is generally a measure of our effort, or time on task. When effectiveness is measured by the number of hours we put in, fatigue is honored. Burnout earns high marks, always. But being busy, even consumed, by the amount of work we do, is a measure of slavery, not freedom; it attends to ego, not purpose.

The Illusion of Control

Control is a way of surrounding ourselves with some measure of certainty that things will turn out the way we think they're supposed to. Sometimes the only way to secure that certainty is by taking care of things yourself. Congregations readily cooperate in this construct: when the challenges facing an organization are too thorny or time-consuming for easy answers, it's easy to hand control over to their pastor or rabbi. "Here, you take charge," they're saying. "Now I can rest." If the leader is reasonably energetic, and even moderately competent, the responsibility is transferred. There is no smaller expectancy of control; it's just in someone else's hands. Often, the leader is happy to take the handoff. Uncertainty can feel more taxing than the tight grip required to keep everything moving in the right direction. But underneath the gloves that dress that grip, our hands are bleeding. Even God relies on partners.

The "I Alone Can Fix This" Identity

Holding power single-handedly is a weighty burden. But its weight is offset by the gravitas it confers. After a while, the yoke is at least familiar, if not comfortable. Leaders know our place in the world by the badge that says we wear an ultimate encumbrance. Our responsibility for the organizations we lead gives us our identity.

A story in the Gospels of the New Testament tells of an encounter Jesus had with a character often described as the rich young ruler (Mark 10:17–31). A young man came to Jesus seeking assurance that he was on the right track. "What must I do to inherit eternal life?" he asked the wise teacher. "Don't you know the standard rules about this?" Jesus asks him (paraphrased). He does. Check. The Gospel writer says, "Jesus looked at him and loved him," which is to say that Jesus understood him. Maybe Jesus identified with the young overachiever. "You are lacking one thing," Jesus said. "Go, sell what you own, and give the money to the poor. Then you will have treasure in heaven. And come, follow me" (Mark 10:21).

The end of the story is unusual in the record for Jesus's failure to close the deal. The invitation to join him, unusually, did not draw an affirmative response. The young man "went away saddened," the Gospel says, "because he had many possessions." This story is too richly nuanced for its meaning to be confined to an obvious point about attachment to money. What Jesus prodded, and what the seeker could not give up, was self-image. Who would the rich young ruler be without the attire—even the weight—of his possessions? It was his identity. Those possessions conferred a package of privileges and responsibilities that gave him his place in the world. The promise of treasure in heaven—the very thing he came to Jesus asking for—could not persuade the young man to let go of what he knew, his familiar burden.

This is the dilemma that many leaders find themselves in. The weight of a singular responsibility for the advancement of their organization is heavy, like the *ephod* (vestment) on the neck of the high priest.[18] Laying it down, pausing for others to step into place, might lighten the load. But the identity that comes with our responsibility is often what holds us in place. Who would we be without our singular burden? For every leader who has been formed in a pyramid culture, there is conscious, intentional, risky work to be done, a different mindset to be cultivated and stewarded, if we are to venture lightly and nimbly into an invitational, less fearful, and more generous life of leadership.

Lighter Luggage

The Changemaker Initiative borrows from the theologian and writer Elaine Heath a spiritual practice she calls the *contemplative stance*, a fourfold rule of life accessible to everyone—activists, contemplatives, everyday faith-seeking folks, and maybe especially leaders:

- Show up
- Pay attention
- Cooperate with God
- Release the outcome[19]

The practice of living daily in this mindful rhythm is a discipline for relinquishing control—not by handing it off but by internalizing the truth that it was never possible to begin with. The contrast is liberating. The stance's deliberate lightness cultivates an openness to the unpredictable. It fosters the wide-open creativity required for innovation. It nurtures curious, open-hearted relationships.

But taking and holding a contemplative stance in the organizations we feel responsible for takes constant, daily practice, consciously setting aside the get-things-done mindset of anxious people and overfunctioning leaders. Every day we have to make the decision to remove from our necks the burdens that have accumulated there overnight, while we weren't paying attention. Every day we can choose a lighter load, depending more trustfully on the people walking alongside us.

▲

Travel Light:
Moses's Story

The Israelites' existential escape from the shadow of the pyramids does not happen overnight; it takes generations. But their physical departure is just that quick. The biblical text spills precious little ink to flesh out the story, but the white lines between the black typeface tell of the Israelites' breathless escape from the centuries-long grasp of their Egyptian captors. Imagine parents waking up children from their innocent slumber, prying the sleep out of their eyes. Picture the frantic darting from corner to corner of their homes, grabbing whatever they could carry. The story is told that they plundered the homes of their Egyptian neighbors, a signal of complete chaos as the tables of power are flipped upside down.

As they run out of their homes, the Israelites take only a few things with them—very few, in fact. Consider, though, what they do not take, what the escaping slaves leave behind. The story does not speak of the precious cooking pot handed down from one generation to the next, the ritual of enslaved mothers feeding their children. Nothing is mentioned of the tattered clothes left in closets and on the floor in the Israelites' hasty exit. And while the story says that they took some unleavened bread with them, we are left to wonder what foods never make the journey.

What the text does tell us, many times over, is that it takes almost no time in the wilderness for the Israelites to yearn for what they left behind in Egypt. They are gripped with nostalgia even before they cross the border. First come the cries to Moses to return them to their slave quarters. The undertow of the status quo is strong, a riptide of fear pulling them back. Distanced from even the meager creature comforts of life in Egypt, the people are sure that death awaits them in the wilderness. They cry out, "What have you done to us, taking us out of Egypt? . . . It is better for us to serve the Egyptians than to die in the wilderness!" (Exod 16:3). As the physical weariness of their desert wandering sets in, they grow thirsty and hungry.[20] They yearn for the corrupted memory of full-bellied days in Egypt. Even if the work was back-breaking, they remember cups that overflowed with fresh water, pots filled with meats and fresh produce. Every day they ate their fill of bread.[21]

By the time the Israelites make it to the other side of the sea that will separate them from the pyramids, their pursuers swept away as the walls of the sea crashed down on them, they have with them only four items of note. Four things are named, carried from their former lives:

- unleavened bread
- gold, silver, and jewels taken from their Egyptian neighbors' homes
- the bones of their ancestor Joseph
- tambourines

They carry only enough to forestall the immediate crisis of the wilderness. Had they tried to bring more bread than fit in their backpacks, it would have risen before its time or spoiled en route. If they had attempted to clean out the Egyptian jewelry coffers, the sheer weight of precious metals would have slowed them down enough to be caught by the army charging behind them. Instead, they carry simple things.

Each of these seemingly unrelated and unessential items carries significance at the surface of the text. Each also offers instruction for our own escape from the contemporary empire's grasp. They are symbols, metaphorical representations of the things we need to escape the confining patterns of leadership imposed by the cultural pharaohs of every generation since liberation from the biblical one. The Israelites' packing list signals what our journey, too, will require:

Sustenance. The Israelites' exodus is a story of liberation. Their freedom is physical, spiritual, and mental. Their bodies are released from hard labor and the abuse of their taskmasters; they are free to worship their God however they please; they will gradually shed the slave's mindset as they journey deeper into the wilderness. But first they have to survive. Dry sand stretches out interminably before them. Their newly liberated bodies needed sustenance to regain and sustain a vigor the wilderness will demand of them. As inspiring as visions of a promised land may be, four centuries of fighting for their lives has kept the Israelites squarely focused on the danger sure to be lurking around the next corner. Starvation is one of them, they know.

Spoils. Beyond bread, they have gathered a small wealth of gold, silver, and jewels to carry with them on their journey. The Israelites have no clear picture of what awaits them on the other side of the exodus; not one of them had ever before left the confines of Egypt. So when they heard the call to gather their things and go, they grabbed from their Egyptian neighbors a few small items of great value. Later, when they arrive in a new home, they suppose, the jewels might be bartered or repurposed. For now, they carry those jewels—symbols of the hope for a better life embedded in the promise of liberation.

The hope of their ancestors. Joseph, grandson of Isaac and great-grandson of Abraham, was the first of the twelve sons who brought their families to Egypt seeking shelter and food. Joseph's last request to his children upon his death was an oath. He implored them to carry his bones with them to his prescient vision of a promised land.[22] Joseph is ancestor to this people, the inheritor and conveyor of God's promise to Abraham to make Abraham's descendants a great nation.

The seventeenth-century commentary Shney Luchot HaBrit says,

> The word for "bones" in Hebrew is the same as the word for "essence"—*etzem.* The Torah's report then has a dual meaning. That is, Moses took Joseph's essence with the Jewish people when they left Egypt. Having acquired Joseph's essence, Moses was later able to give the Jewish people the Torah.[23]

And so, as Moses prepares to take the Israelites out of Egypt four centuries later, he painstakingly tracks down Joseph's coffin,[24] answering the promise that had been passed down for generations. Relics in his hands, Moses carefully plans for safe transit of this ancestor's legacy. Joseph's hope, his ambition for his children and grandchildren and great-grandchildren, will travel with them as the people carry his bones. They will deliver the bones to the place of final burial Joseph hoped for,[25] not so much for the sake of the bones themselves but so the essence of Joseph—his legacy, the tradition he embodies—will remain with them.

The sound of celebration. Of all the useful things she could have picked up as she grabbed what she could before rushing out, Miriam, Moses's sister, packs timbrels, ancient precursors to tambourines. And she holds them tight. She doesn't drop them as she runs from the Egyptian chariots steadily gaining ground on the ragged band of refugees. She clings to them as she steps onto the miraculously dry land between two imposing walls of water. And once she makes it to safety, even the thunderous crash of the waters behind her does not loosen her grip on the instruments. Miriam knows that at some point, their bodies will need to dance, to sing and celebrate in ways that they could never do while shackled in Egypt. Miriam's decision to pack timbrels defines the character she is remembered for. She is known for her righteousness,[26] a faith that never wavers during the Israelites' break for freedom. She is Miriam the prophetess,[27] titled for her faithful forethought that wherever the Israelites are headed, there will be cause for celebration. What Miriam holds in her hands, what she carries for all of them, is more than hope; it is promise. Promise of better days ahead. Promise of joy, even in the midst of profound tumult. Promise of the permanence of God's love, even when it is not quite visible.[28]

Perhaps exodus and liberation are cyclical. Every generation is both uplifted by its predecessors and wriggling free of their grasp. This generation is not the first to know the need for resourcefulness and pragmatism. The difficulty distinguishing between the ancestral identity we are bound to carry with us and the trappings of tradition we are being invited to leave behind is as real for us as it was for Moses. The dilemma's theological implications are profound. Religion is defined by the story it does not make up but participates in. We are the inheritors of promises we are bound to sustain, beyond our ability to visualize their usefulness or current relevance. The question for leaders who are willing to shed tradition for transformation is, What are those timeless, essential promises? And what, beyond them, shall we leave behind?

Notes

1 This saying was coined by the management guru Peter Drucker in 2006 and made famous by Mark Fields, who later became chief executive of Ford Motor Company.

2 Rashi (Rabbi Shlomo Yitzhaki) was an eleventh-century French rabbi and prolific commentator on, among other texts, Torah and Talmud.

3 "Moving the goalposts" is a form of psychologically manipulative control in which the abuser initially gives one set of directions, and then—after the victim completes them—changes the directions, usually making the task more difficult for the victim. Not only does it make their work harder, but it forces them to question their own memory of the initial demand.

4 Adam Kligfeld, interview, June 22, 2022.

5 Kligfeld, interview.

6 Kligfeld, interview.

7 Kligfeld, interview.

8 Kligfeld, interview.

9 Rabbinic texts offer a range of ages for girls to become bat mitzvah, from twelve to twelve and a half to thirteen.

10 Kligfeld, interview.

11 Kligfeld, interview.

12 Quoted in Jenna Krajeski, "This Is Water," *New Yorker*, September 19, 2008, https://tinyurl.com/5x45dkum.

13 This notion of feeling chased, or chasing something else, calls to mind an important teaching from the Babylonian Talmud, Eruvin 13b: "This is to teach you that anyone who humbles themselves, the Holy One, Blessed be God, exalts them, and anyone who exalts themselves, the Holy One, Blessed be God, humbles them. Anyone who seeks greatness, greatness flees from them, and, conversely, anyone who flees from greatness, greatness seeks them. And anyone who attempts to force the moment and expends great effort to achieve an objective precisely when they desire to do so, the moment forces them back, too, and they are unsuccessful. And conversely, anyone who is patient and yields to the moment, the moment abides, and they will ultimately be successful."

14 This quote is usually attributed to Mark Zuckerberg, founder of Facebook, from early in the social media company's explosive success.

15 Several of these studies are documented in Matt Bloom, *Flourishing in Ministry: How to Cultivate Clergy Wellbeing* (Lanham, MD: Rowman & Littlefield, 2019).

16 Thomas R. Steagold, "I'm Finally Taking My First Sabbatical from Ministry," *The Christian Century*, August 7, 2016, https://tinyurl.com/2p967xwh.

17 Brené Brown, *The Gifts of Imperfection: Let Go of Who You Think You're Supposed to Be and Embrace Who You Are*, anniversary ed. (Center City, MN: Hazelden, 2022).

18 Interestingly, while the high priest donned the ephod, rabbinic commentary in the Tosefta notes that he was supported on both sides by priestly underlings in order to bear the tremendous weight of the jewels. He got the credit for the holiness it conferred, but he did not bear its weight alone.

19 Elaine Heath, *God Unbound: Wisdom from Galatians for the Anxious Church* (Nashville: Upper Room Books, 2016), chap. 5.

20 Exod 15:24: "And the people grumbled against Moses, saying, 'What shall we drink?'" Again at Exod 17:3: "But the people thirsted there for water; and the people grumbled against Moses and said, 'Why did you bring us up from Egypt, to kill us and our children and livestock with thirst?'"

21 Num 11:4–6: "The riffraff in their midst felt a gluttonous craving; and then the Israelites wept and said, 'If only we had meat to eat! We remember the fish that we used to eat free in Egypt, the cucumbers, the melons, the leeks, the onions, and the garlic. Now our gullets are shriveled. There is nothing at all! Nothing but this manna to look to!'"

22 Gen 50:25–26: "And Joseph took an oath of the children of Israel, saying: 'God will surely remember you, and ye shall carry up my bones from hence.' So Joseph died, being a hundred and ten years old. And they embalmed him, and he was put in a coffin in Egypt."

23 Shney Luchot HaBrit, Torah Ohr 111. Composed in Ottoman Palestine (ca. 1611–ca. 1631). Written by Rabbi Isaiah HaLevi Horovitz (ca. 1555–1630), who is known by the acronym of the title of the book (Shelah).

24 According to a midrash on the episode of Moses tracking down Joseph's bones, Serah daughter of Asher instructed Moses to go to the brink of the Nile and beseech God to help him fulfill Joseph's last request. Immediately, Joseph's coffin rose up from the depths of the Nile just within reach of Moses.

25 Josh 24:32: "And the bones of Joseph, which the children of Israel brought up out of Egypt, buried they in Shechem, in the parcel of ground which Jacob bought of the sons of Hamor the father of Shechem for a hundred pieces of money; and they became the inheritance of the children of Joseph."

26 "The righteous women in that generation were confident that God would perform miracles for them, and they accordingly had brought timbrels with them from Egypt" (Mekhilta d'Rabbi Yishmael).

27 Exod 15:20–21: "Then Miriam the prophetess, Aaron's sister, took a timbrel in her hand, and all the women went out after her, dancing with timbrels. And Miriam chanted for them: Sing to Adonai, for God has triumphed gloriously."

28 While Miriam's timbrels only seem to have made it as far as she did, the tradition of celebrating with song and dance became a critical part of the Israelites' evolution into a nation, both in the wilderness and in the promised land. We see mentions of timbrels a number of times after the Israelites cross the border, from King David to Jephtheh's daughter, from Judges to Job. Miriam did not just inspire one song, one dance, in one particularly jubilant moment. She wasn't just carrying a musical instrument. She modeled a way of leading into uncertainty, open-hearted and unabashedly hopeful. She carried in her hands the ambitions of a newly free nation, which not only fueled them in the moment but carried them for generations to come.

CHAPTER SIX

Liberating Structures

Everyone familiar with brainstorming sessions knows that they often devolve into less brain and more storm. These are the meetings where everyone is seated in their normal spots around a table. Whoever is chairing the meeting (usually the most senior person in the room, usually sitting at the head of the table) charges the group with the task of coming up with ingenious ideas for new programs. But as pure of heart as the invitation may have been, it falls flat. The group grinds through a list of minor tweaks to current routines; nothing sounds new enough or worth the effort of change.[1]

More often than not, the obstacle in the room is not any single person or even a collective failure of creativity. It's an invisible but powerful chorus of uninvited voices. They're an indistinguishable and often unattributable mix of nostalgic yearnings that grumble, "But we've always done it this way," a fearful resistance that is quick to point out, "That'll never work." But often there's a detectable shadow in the room even more powerful than nostalgia or resistance.

Look closely. Typically, the less senior folks in the room are being urged to come up with ideas to meet the goals of the most senior ones. The pressure to please the powerful reverberates throughout the room. It shuts down daring conversation before it even begins. So the ideas that emerge from such brainstorming tend to be the ones that most closely resemble exactly what you're already doing, just shinier. Worship—now with electric guitars!

This is the challenge of unexamined power. Unrecognized and unaddressed, it simultaneously holds back those who own it and shuts down those who are governed by it. It is the pink elephant in the room doing its very best to evade attention until it decides to rear up and make its presence known in a word that suddenly sounds like a veto, not a vote. It's the senior pastor who amicably invites you to "Call me Joe" until the context changes without warning and suddenly, in public, he's "Pastor Smith" to you, too.

Power is often invisible, or at least well-hidden. But it is an inescapable and necessary thing. It's also a malleable thing, capable of being passed, divided, shared. When it is held only atop an organization, rather than flowing freely throughout, it's not just brainstorming sessions that suffer; it's the people too. In our preference for predictability, we often reinforce our organizational structures without thinking about the effect of all that cement. The same buttresses that support a stable order hold our feet in place when we want them to move, when the dancing music begins.

On Strategy and Culture

A *Harvard Business Review* article analyzed multiple field studies and concluded that somewhere between 60 and 90 percent of strategic plans never fully launch.[2] These studies surveyed some of the largest companies in the world, which, in turn, hired some of the largest consulting firms in the world to develop their strategic plans. So these were the priciest strategic plans the consulting world has to offer, prepared by some of the smartest business minds educated by the ivy-est of Ivy League business schools. And only a small percentage of them actually work. McKinsey and Company, one of those elite consulting firms, shared a similar report about the success (or lack thereof) of its strategic plans.[3] It disclosed a number of important insights gleaned from the research, and it was refreshingly straightforward about its failures.

One client, Royalfield Company,[4] was led by officers who hired strategic-planning consultants but didn't understand the meaning of the word *strategy* or the process through which the company's strategy would be created. It's no surprise, then, that 70 percent of the company's executives did not like the strategic planning process, and 70 percent of its board members didn't trust the results.[5] Other companies demonstrated similar dissatisfaction with the outcomes of consulting services they had paid tens—sometimes hundreds—of thousands of dollars for. They cited lack of transparent communication, mistrust across the organization, too much focus on ends and not enough on means, and the catchall: company culture.

Perhaps the most striking feature of this report is that the people surveyed about the effectiveness of McKinsey's strategic-planning services were the *same ones* who had initiated the consultation. It wasn't resistance throughout the organization that undermined the strategic plan's implementation; it was the culture of the company itself—culture that is set at the top of the organizational chart. An organization's orientation to strategic planning, or new ideas, or change in general, cascades down to the employees tasked with the plan's day-to-day implementation, but it does not originate there. Most staff members go into strategic change processes with goodwill and an earnest embrace of organizational mission. But that goodwill is delicate; it is easily broken. When it is imposed on to support the weighty layers of management focused on sustaining their own rank, it cracks quickly.

Organizations that are agile enough to absorb change tend to be organizations conscious that their culture is supple, always in a state of reformation, day in and day out. They don't turn reflexively to established regulations or protocols that cover every possibility. They allow themselves to shapeshift a little, bending one way or another as the moment calls on them to do.

Structures That Nurture Culture

In 2013, a book by Henri Lipmanowicz and Keith McCandless called *The Surprising Power of Liberating Structures* made its way onto thousands of bookshelves in dozens of countries. The book is chock-full of inspiring stories of organizational change, leadership growth, and breakthrough ideas based on years of research and lived experience. Its unique contribution to leadership at every level of every organization is the simplicity of the structures it proposes to disentangle organizations that have gotten mired in their complexity.

The irony embedded in the book's wisdom is that the structures referred to in the title are not structures at all; they're temporary frameworks, tiny shifts in the way that employees meet, plan, decide, and relate to one another. Like the ancient Israelites' tabernacle, these tent-like structures go up when the time is right, and they're easily disassembled when it's time to move on. They're sturdy enough to withstand the organization's leaning on them and agile enough to relocate when necessary. It's the word *liberating* that delineates these structures. It is their very impermanence, incompleteness, and simplicity that frees both leaders and organizational team members to do—and be—their best.[6]

> At the core . . . is the practical idea that simple shifts in our routine patterns of interaction make it possible for everyone to be included, engaged, and unleashed in solving problems, driving innovation, and achieving extraordinary outcomes. Small changes generate big results without important best practices, more training, or expensive buy-in strategies.
>
> Liberating structures are quite simple and easy to learn; they can be used by everyone at every level, from the C-suite to the front line of any organization, from the neighborhood block club to the global issue-advocacy association. . . . Everyday use in a conversation or meeting can be as powerful as application to the big transformation initiative.[7]

While Lipmanowicz and McCandless offer dozens of examples of these structures, they all take their shape from a very simple idea: if you create the context for everyone in the room to bring their gifts to bear, the rest is just details. Breakthrough creativity thrives with some constraints; the challenge for an organization's leaders is to design and host a process that is clear enough to inspire inventiveness and still flexible enough to unleash both individual ingenuity and collective wisdom. When everyone shows up fully, feels respected completely, and experiences themselves as truly free, the power of the group becomes unleashed.

We often think of change as starting from the top down or the bottom up. An organizational pyramid is either upright or inverted.[8] But truly liberating structures invite change from every position, including from the outside in. Many of the stories shared by the *Liberating Structures* authors describe transformation that has taken place in schools, communities, and organizations when the least empowered individuals have been invited to share their gifts and step into power, even if only temporarily.

Who are those folks in your community, your neighborhood, even your family? The ones on the periphery, the ones who hold back, the ones who have come to accept their station in the back of the room, the ones who may never say out loud what it is they yearn for. What would it look like to place them at the center of the story, even if just for a moment? To treat their stories like Scripture, their perspectives as prophecy? What might you stand to learn from them? Imagine, just for a moment, how it might make them feel to be witnessed with eagerness and love.

There is risk in replacing sturdy structures with fungible frameworks, even temporarily. Placing new voices at the center of organizational life demands that other voices step back. The edifice might sway a little. People might get anxious. It might get messy. But liberation is a big promise.

Rethinking Power: Maurice Winley's Story

You don't have to hear Reverend Maurice Winley preach to know that he is blessed with the pointed wisdom of a prophet. He sees opportunity that others overlook, possibility in the most unlikely places. And he's not afraid to challenge accepted truths. In fact, in Winley's first homework assignment in an entrepreneurship fellowship,[9] he challenged the underlying assumption of the assignment itself. His task—to fill out an organizational chart for the organization that Winley was in the process of building—had been completed by hundreds of students before him, each of whom followed the instructions and filled in the little boxes, their own name almost always at the very top. But not Winley.

Winley's submission had none of those boxes, and it took a very different shape from the pyramid-like structure outlined in the assignment. He submitted a beautifully composed, oval-shaped chart, with photos of each of his team members in their element, serving their community. From the very moment that Winley founded the Living Redemption Youth Opportunity Hub, he was rethinking traditional patterns of organizational power and hierarchy, and for good reason. He knew from personal experience just how painful it is to feel powerless. He wanted his organization to ensure that nobody in his orbit would ever have to go through what he did.

A judge told me at the age of seventeen that I was a cancer to society because of the decisions I had made. Now, I'm there for serious charges; I knew that. But at the same time, I'm seventeen years old! For every decision we make, there's a multiplicity of things that have transpired to bring us to that moment. I saw the abuses of power [in the New York State prison system], I experienced the kind of powerlessness where you can't speak, when you're walked through a hall in silence, underneath a tower with weapons aimed at you, when you're getting strip-searched. That's powerlessness.[10]

By the time he was released from prison at the age of twenty-one, Winley had experienced more heartache than many folks do in a lifetime. He embraced the newfound freedom of his release enthusiastically, but he wasn't satisfied with a world in which so many young Black men from Harlem faced the potential for that same heartache, or worse. So, as he began rebuilding his life as a young adult, Winley heard the first inkling of a call into faith leadership. It was a very specific calling; he knew that whatever form his ministry would take, he would never stray far from the community he came from, the community that needed him most. He knows:

> There are seven neighborhoods in New York City where 80 percent of the entire New York State Penitentiary population was coming from.[11] Just seven neighborhoods! And Harlem was one of them. The reality of that fact affects everything: poverty, the disruption to the family, educational outcomes, health outcomes, mental health. It impacts the totality of individuals' lives, and those of their families. This is paramount to my work.[12]

Start with Self

Living Redemption, the organization Winley started, is built on a very simple notion: every person has a unique story to tell and priceless gifts to give, and every person deserves an opportunity (and sometimes multiple opportunities) to share them. Before he could lead an organization that lives into those values, Winley needed to go through a deep process of reflecting on his own fraught relationship with systems of power. He often advises others to start with themselves if they want to see change in the world. He had to do the same thing.

First, he wanted to ensure that he did not perpetuate the damaging, coercive power dynamics that he'd experienced in the criminal justice system. "I feel that the first power shift we have to make is internal. It's about our relationship to love, faith, hope, our relationship to God, versus our relationship to the desires of self. That's the first realm of power struggle. All of the systems we see that operate like dominant, transactional imperialism—those are an expression of what's inside of each of us."[13]

Second, he sought to guard himself against the danger of his own mistrustful leadership. "How do we override our natural inclinations toward distrust on an everyday basis?" he asks. "The journey that God has led me to has been through the wilderness of my soul. My work now is to bring others into the promised land that I've been able to witness. I'm still on that journey."[14]

Finally, he knew that if Living Redemption was to be successful, it would have to partner with some of the same systems that had failed him as a young man. That meant that Winley needed to be clear-eyed and open-hearted about approaching the possibility of partnership with people and institutions that had hurt him before. He could try to change the systems because he hated them, but it would be far more effective if he worked to change the systems because he loved the people affected by them. This shift in thinking was one of astounding spiritual proportions. "You have to guard your heart, particularly when you are in a position of power. You have to humble yourself. And sometimes you have to be very tolerant. You have to be very patient. But at the same time you have to tell the truth. You have to speak with both truth and love, at the same time. Truth spoken without love is one of the most destructive things on this planet."[15]

Credible Messengers

In the first days of his work, Winley assembled a cadre of people whom he called credible messengers. These were people who had gone through the criminal justice system themselves. They would act as mentors, intervening in the lives of their counterparts, young men who looked like them and who might, without intervention, be headed toward a similar fate. Now, there are lots of initiatives aimed at breaking the school-to-prison pipeline. But most depend on outside, so-called experts to steer young men in the right direction. Winley knew that the expertise that could make a difference was not a diploma on a wall or a certificate of completion from some training program. What mattered was the mentor's own lived experience. In Winley's neighborhood in Harlem, those kinds of experts were plentiful, and they were just waiting to be seen.

Building a team of folks with the kinds of experience Winley was looking for—people who had been wrapped up in the criminal justice system, who had made the kinds of mistakes Winley wanted to prevent others from making, who had fallen victim to the intertwined failures of the school, public health, and justice systems—would be complicated. If this thing was going to have real impact, it needed to be built around people just like him, real people with gritty, mostly unappreciated personal experience. This is what would make them transformative mentors to the people who needed their encouragement most.

Winley's ambitious vision required a long view, a commitment not to exchange impact for efficiency or humanity for headlines. When we think only about our personal agendas, he says, "It results in a loss of trust. And so we haven't represented God well. We lose the investment of love, faith, hope that has been entrusted to us. We no longer embody and express the reality of God because we really have become fixated on the temporal. This is the great exchange. The temporal versus eternal."[16]

When Winley invited those credible messengers into the transcendent work he imagined for them, he started by doing something the criminal justice system had failed to do for him: he reminded them of their infinite value, restored them to their dignity, dreamed with them about the promises ahead. He knew what they sometimes could not see for themselves: that God loved them, mistakes and all, and that they were worthy to do God's work in the world. He knew this because he once had to be convinced of those same truths: "I have experienced God's grace. I got it by His truth and His spirit. That's what overcame those internal pains. . . . There's a freedom and grace that we obtain. There's also a boldness when we really come to understand that we have been forgiven, that we have been redeemed."[17]

Winley's vision did not happen immediately. It took patience and persistence for the credible messengers to realize for themselves the profound experience of feeling forgiven. It took time for them to feel their own power to share that grace with others. But Winley had one honest conversation, made one bold invitation, issued one provocative challenge at a time. He patiently built the first team of credible messengers, the first four employees at Living Redemption Youth Opportunity Hub. A decade later, each of those four now serves in a director role in the organization.

The longevity of their tenure is a testament to the ways that Winley has given them space to grow into their gifts. He didn't give them a script on their first day or a blueprint for how to engage young people in their neighborhoods. He did the slow work of witnessing their stories, helping them see their own gifts, and inviting them to hold their own power. "We are big on mobilizing, empowering each credible messenger. We believe they have a unique value proposition. I tell 'em that everybody here is a kung fu specialist. 'You have a unique form of kung fu, something that nobody else here can do. With all the challenges you've overcome, with all your gifts, there's something that only you represent. Our job is to liberate those gifts and bring them to life.'"

Time, Talent, Treasure, and Trust

With his team firmly in place and his organization growing steadily, the demands on Winley's time soon began to increase beyond his capacity. He found himself often in interviews with the press, in meetings with city officials, on grant-maker site visits. Winley grew concerned that his limited bandwidth might bottleneck the organization. If he held on to too much power himself, the organization would grind to a halt. If he was the only person qualified to handle certain responsibilities, the others would wait around until he tended to them. If his salary was too high, there would be no room in the budget for others to thrive. And if he were the sole face of the organization, outsiders would never come to trust his colleagues.

Winley had named Living Redemption intentionally. He saw himself as part of a living, breathing ecosystem. If the organization was going to sustain itself, power—in all its forms—needed to flow freely to and from each individual inside it. So Winley put this idea into practice in every facet of the organization's operations. When it came time for important decisions about the organization's budget, the deployment of employees' time, engaging with outside partners, or building new capacities, he spent the time discerning with his team the next steps forward. He had learned to hold power like the manna that appeared as food to the Israelites in the wilderness. You take just as much as you need for this day. If you take more, it will rot, and it will rob others of what they need for their own sustenance: "There were times where I had the opportunity to get salary increases, but I gave it to the team. I didn't broadcast it, but I knew it was the right thing to do. I chose to do that; I was following God's roadmap for me, with integrity and innovation. I believe that this model of sharing is the missing ingredient in our world today."[18]

The same patient culture that Winley set for Living Redemption in its nascency still characterized its life ten years later. Living Redemption developed generative relationships with grant makers and partnerships with criminal justice and educational systems. In its first decade, credible messengers served 109,039 individuals.[19] Every person engaged in Living Redemption's mission is entrusted to own a place in the holy work the organization is about, to tell their story, and to hold the power they need to bring into the world a lasting redemption—their own, that of the people who have already passed through the Hub's hallways, and that of those who have not yet arrived.

Winley is beginning to see glimpses of the system-wide change that he has dreamed about for years.

> As we developed relationships with key partners, we realized we were speaking of and sharing the same core values. From there, we affirmed them with those values, and vice versa. And it just brought us closer, closer, closer. That felt very profound. When we were working with, for example, the New York City Department of Probation, from the Commissioner level all the way down to the probation level, I could start to see some incremental change. I have to keep remembering that the type of change and the transformation that we desire to see is not microwavable. It is a very slow process.[20]

Light Attracts Light

At fifty, Winley reflected on the power that this work has given him to be a changemaker in his community and in the world. He is bold about imagining what God might do next through Living Redemption. But often, his mind's eye goes back to the dark, dank, one-room office where it all started, and the critical lesson he learned inside of those four walls.

> This was a very volatile time. Our assignment was to work with young men coming out of West Harlem . . . that was the name of the program, West Harlem Transformative Mentoring. That's where we started. As the young space became sacred, it was just a room on the sixth floor of a building. But that space became illuminated because of the people who entered it. Anyone who walked in could experience the living ethos

that was vibrating through the room, through that space. You saw it immediately: light attracts light, and that same light repels darkness, too.[21]

Just Enough:
Moses's Story

On the other side of the Red Sea, as memories of the exultant dancing led by Miriam's tambourines fade, the Israelites' sense of foreboding returns. The pyramids might be far behind, but the memory of enslavement is not. Its taste lingers on their tongues; wounds from their taskmasters' whips haven't yet scarred over. Invigorated by God's word and inspiration, Moses might imagine the wilderness ahead as pregnant with possibility, but the Israelites see only a barren wasteland. Moses dreams; they are dismayed.

The invincible Egyptians must still be chasing them, they imagine, even from the other side of the sea. The Egyptian army is strong; its warriors will find a way to come after us, the people worry. Their fear, their knowledge of how things always work, is deeply embedded. And mostly their worries have been justified—as far back as their historical memory can stretch. Their pessimism drowns out the hope that had ever so briefly stirred among them as the waters of the sea parted for them, by some miracle they cannot explain.

"Get up," Moses says. "We have to keep going." They travel for three days, the Exodus narrative says, without water. They are parched, weary. The landscape is unfamiliar. They come to a stream—finally!—and set up camp, but the water is bitter and undrinkable (Exod 15:23). "Marah," they name the place. It means "bitterness"—for the water and perhaps for the people's mood. They rail against Moses. His leadership must be deficient if this is where they have arrived. There is another small miracle; Moses appeals to God, and the water is made sweet.

But the respite is short-lived. This latest miracle holds off their grumbling for only a short while. They soon camp in Elim, where there are—surprise!—not one but twelve springs of water and seventy palm trees (Exod 15:27). Even there they cannot tarry; they continue on their way, only to begin complaining to Moses and Aaron once again. In the wilderness of Sinai's desert, their hunger overwhelms them, and their nostalgia for the full food pots of Egypt beckons them into the past. "If only we had died by the hand of God in the land of Egypt, when we sat by the fleshpots, when we ate our fill of bread! For you have brought us out into this wilderness to starve this whole congregation to death" (Exod 16:3).

Certain that death is near, they accuse Moses of taking away what little comfort they once had and replacing it with endless meandering through the wilderness on empty stomachs and with parched throats.

But there is another miracle. God rains nourishment on them, in the mysterious form of *manna*. Whatever it is, it fills their stomachs, in the form of quail by night and bread by morning. But there is a strange set of rules governing its collection.

Each evening, quail appears before them and covers the camp with enough sustenance for each mouth present. And every morning, "When the fall of dew lifted, there, over the surface of the wilderness, lay a fine and flaky substance, as fine as frost on the ground" (Exod 16:14). Like so much of what will sustain the Israelites in time, the manna is almost invisible; it's an act of faith just imagining that it will meet their hands when they reach to scoop it up each morning.

Even more curiously, this heavenly manna seems to anticipate the intentions of its bearers. If they aim to hoard it for a midnight snack, taking even slightly more than their share, the manna spoils and becomes infested. And for those who delay in their gathering, who will not take what they need at the opportune time, it melts by the heat of the sun and leaves them empty-handed. The manna tolerates neither greed nor sloth;

they are to take what they need, when they need it. Nothing more, and nothing less. Manna is a temporary solution to an urgent hunger. Like the tabernacle they will carry with them to house the presence of their God, manna is meant to be a liberating structure, not a lasting edifice against hunger.

But all the rules yield to the centrality of the Sabbath. For six un-Sabbathed days, leftover manna turns into maggot food. But on the Sabbath, it remains. On the Sabbath's eve they collect double portions, so they might prepare, baking and boiling the sustenance they will need for the coming day of rest, confident that God, in all of God's idiosyncrasies, has provided another fashion of nourishment on the holy day ahead.

Hungry no more, the Israelites delight in their miraculous new food. It tastes "like wafers in honey" (Exod 16:31). For a time, it quells their anxiety about the road ahead. "And the Israelites ate manna for forty years, until they came to a settled land; they ate the manna until they came to the border of the land of Canaan" (Exod 16:35).

It is, of course, not only the manna itself that fuels their journey and shapes their becoming. It's the lessons underlying this powerful substance. Moses learns, alongside the Israelites, that all God grants—food, water, even power—is an infinite resource when it is received with faith that there is more where it came from. But there are correspondent commitments on the part of the receiver: the humility to take only what is needed in the moment, the circumspection to notice the needs of others while assessing your own. To stash any more than that is to take what has been offered as liberation and fold it back into that familiar pyramid shape all over again.

Notes

1   On church brainstorms: How is it possible that, with all of the smart people sitting around the table, the best anyone came up with was "Funny Tie Fridays"?

2 Andrea Belk Olson, "4 Common Reasons Strategies Fail," *Harvard Business Review*, June 24, 2022, https://tinyurl.com/37x8fzj6.

3 Tera Allas, Louis Chambers, and Tom Welchman, "Confronting Overconfidence in Talent Strategy, Management, and Development," McKinsey Review, June 20, 2019, https://tinyurl.com/3djcphxr.

4 This is a pseudonym for an S&P 500 company, to protect its identity.

5 Chris Bradley, Martin Hirt, and Sven Smit, "Strategy to Beat the Odds," *McKinsey Quarterly*, February 13, 2018, https://tinyurl.com/5kcx4eu2.

6 For example, Lipmanowicz and McCandless suggest replacing conventional brainstorming sessions with a format more hospitable to small, risk-taking ideas. Calling it 1-2-4-All, they propose:

    - Silent self-reflection by individuals on a shared challenge, framed as a question (e.g., What opportunities do YOU see for making progress on this challenge? How would you handle this situation? What ideas or actions do you recommend?) 1 min.
    - Generate ideas in pairs, building on ideas from self-reflection. 2 min.
    - Share and develop ideas from your pair in foursomes (notice similarities and differences). 4 min.
    - Ask, "What is one idea that stood out in your conversation?" Each group shares one important idea with all (repeat cycle as needed). 5 min.

    "1-2-4-All," Liberating Structures, https://tinyurl.com/2vkvwwxj.

7 Henri Lipmanowicz and Keith McCandless, *The Surprising Power of Liberating Structures: Simple Rules to Unleash a Culture of Innovation* (n.p.: Liberating Structures, 2014), 4.

8 See Michael M. Canaris, "The Pope's 'Inverted Pyramid' Vision of the Church," *Catholic Star Press*, August 2, 2018, https://tinyurl.com/46yk8t33.

9 Glean Network's Start Fellowship, which partners with Columbia Business School, www.gleannetwork.org/start.

10 Maurice Winley, interview, November 17, 2022.

11 "The Seven Neighborhood Study Revisited," Center for NuLeadership, 2013, https://tinyurl.com/3cbcfp2m.

12 Winley, interview.

13 Winley, interview.

14 Winley, interview.

15 Winley, interview.

16 Winley, interview.

17 Winley, interview.

18 Winley, interview.

19 Living Redemption, https://livingredemption.org/.

20 Winley, interview.

21 Winley, interview.

CHAPTER SEVEN

Testing for Trust

Most leaders know that they can trust themselves. They may second-guess their own decisions from time to time, but somewhere along the way, with their own or others' affirmation, they have internalized a reliable expectation that they will do the right thing. In *The Currency of Connection*, the leadership consultant Teresa Mitrovic says self-trust is characterized by a handful of traits that demonstrate a powerful core of confidence:

- Knowing that the beliefs you hold are consistently expressed through your behavior;
- Knowing your behavior will be consistent, no matter who you are with or what pressure you are under;
- Having the courage to try, and to make mistakes;
- Being honest about your mistakes and choosing candor, humility, and learning in the face of shame or embarrassment;
- Extending compassion and care to the people you work and live with even when you know it may not be reciprocated;
- Appreciating that you are making the best decisions you can at the time you're making them, even if things look different with hindsight.[1]

Self-trust is what allows leaders to move their convictions into action. It emboldens them to speak and act with the kind of strength that inspires others to follow. Self-trust gives leaders a sense of safety even when the external environment is full of danger. That's true for everyone: someone else's trust in you offers the safety and courage to act.

Stephen M. Covey reports that in organizations with a high-trust culture, people are thirty-two times more likely to take a responsible risk than they are in a low-trust culture. They're eleven times more likely to innovate and six times more likely to achieve high performance.[2] Neuroscientist Paul Zak finds that "compared with people at low-trust companies, people at high-trust companies report 74% less stress, 106% more energy at work, 50% higher productivity, 13% fewer sick days, 76% more engagement, 29% more satisfaction with their lives, 40% less burnout."[3]

When trust flows liberally, so many valuable resources are spread: power, hope, care, confidence. All of us might acknowledge this ideal in the abstract; if we are blessed, we might have seen it at work in a small way, perhaps with a few close colleagues or confidants. But getting trust to flow abundantly through an organization is not an obvious proposition.

Even the most secure pyramid leader knows intuitively that others' trust in them makes the system work better. Trust in others demands risk taking. Sometimes it requires letting go of things that seemingly prudent leaders are inclined to hold onto: reliance on our own expertise, self-sufficiency, even well-grounded fear. This is why trust is often encased in the pyramid's top floor. Leaders may trust themselves and possibly those in their inner circle, but everyone else is regarded as if their commitment and energy and personal investment were suspect. But one-directional trust is a fragile thing. In the ancient wise words of Lao Tzu, "He who does not trust enough will not be trusted."[4] Mutual trust—the kind that allows organizations and their people to thrive as they take risks together—demands the willingness of those in power to wade into the wilderness, to relinquish control over outcomes, and to live comfortably alongside the uncertainty that trusting others inevitably brings.

What Keeps You Up at Night? Elan's Story

In 2008, I began working as a community organizer with the Industrial Areas Foundation (IAF) affiliate in Los Angeles, OneLA.[5] My supervisor, Sister Maribeth Larkin, set a goal for me of forty one-to-one meetings per week. One-to-ones are the single most important tool of an Industrial Areas Foundation organizer; they help us learn the stories of each neighborhood, to sync up with the heartbeat of churches, synagogues, mosques, and schools as we try to build a powerful, broad-based coalition.

Those one-to-ones were so critical to this work, in fact, that most of my early supervision meetings with Maribeth were simply about troubleshooting ways for me to somehow find forty people willing to meet with me and picking the right Los Angeles roads to get to those meetings on time. In those early weeks I felt like I could manage eight to fifteen meetings a week. Forty seemed utterly impossible. For one, I was—and am—committed to the observance of Shabbat, so that left me with six days to identify potential meeting prospects, schedule them, and navigate the purgatory of Los Angeles traffic. I spent most of my driving time in first gear in the parking lots known as the 10, the 405, and the 101.[6]

But the real obstacle wasn't just traffic; it was trust—something I wasn't doing a great job of earning. The truth is that I wasn't all that good at facilitating those meetings. When I closed with the question, "Who else should I talk to in this community?" I usually got crickets back. Absent any referrals coming from these initial one-to-ones, there was no way I was ever going to pan out as an organizer.

A few months in, I met Carlos (not his real name) at a church cookout in Mid-City. He was curious about the *kippah*-wearing man speaking barely passable Spanish, so he accepted my invitation for a coffee later that week. We met at a greasy-spoon diner close to where he lived with his family, just two blocks from his childhood home. When the server, whom he knew by name, came to take our orders, we both ordered black coffees. I was drinking so much coffee each week that it seemed health-conscious to at least give up cream and sugar. I thanked Carlos for taking the time to meet with me.

With great pride of place, Carlos shared a few of his childhood memories of the neighborhood and how happy he was to see it flourishing of late. Many of the small bungalow homes had been renovated inside and out, and he was thrilled to have been able to buy one for his family. Best of all, he noted, so many locally owned businesses like this diner were succeeding. He hoped it was a sign that the neighborhood might thrive.

As a community organizer, though, my job was about more than witnessing the bright spots; I had to seek out the pain points of the neighborhood, too. And once I identified those, then I had to go out and find people ready to work to address them. If Carlos had only good news to share, I wondered why he had agreed to meet with me. And something else didn't quite make sense. If his rosy reports were true, his family was healthy and well, his business was in the black, and his house was pristine, why did he look like he hadn't slept in days? With the clock ticking down on our time together, I decided to just go for it.

"Carlos, what's keeping you up at night?"

At first, he brushed off the question. "Nothing. Nothing at all." I kept quiet, letting the silence invite more. He tensed, determined to keep it light. "Sure, I'd be happier if the Lakers didn't lose so much. And it would be great if the police sirens weren't so loud at night, but they're doing what they can to keep us safe." I nodded my head but stayed silent for another beat. So did he. And then he closed his eyes, took in a deep breath, and sighed loudly, like he was steeling himself. He gathered his coffee mug in both hands, and leaned forward, sharing quietly:

Okay, you're right. I do have a reason that I wanted to talk to you because I don't know what to do about something. You see, a few years ago, when I was going through the process of applying for a mortgage, I messed up. Even though I probably could have been approved for a normal, thirty-year loan, the lender kept selling me on a lower rate. He showed me the calculations of what I could save with this other loan he was offering, and it was crazy. Like hundreds and hundreds of dollars a month cheaper. It was too good to pass up.

But a few months ago, I got a letter from the bank saying that I had a new payment amount—more than twice what I was paying before. I was sure it was a mistake. So I went into the bank the next day, spoke with three different people including the manager, and they all said the same thing: this was how my kind of mortgage worked and the new payment amount was correct. So now I'm three months late on those bigger payments, and the letters from the bank are getting more and more serious, like I could lose my house if I don't do something.

His story shocked me. Carlos had just told me he was the owner of a successful business, that his family donated to the clothing drives at his church regularly, that he volunteered as a reading buddy at the neighborhood elementary school in his spare time. How could this man seemingly so secure in every way be just weeks away from losing his home?

Carlos was one of millions of Americans who had been duped by the corporate lenders that launched the country into the subprime mortgage crisis and the deepest recession in generations. Only a small handful of the bankers who caused this crisis ended up behind bars. But a staggering number of the homeowners they defrauded lost their homes and their families' hope to be part of the American dream of home ownership. That's what kept Carlos up at night. That was the root of his restlessness.

I explained to Carlos that this was a new issue for the IAF and that we might not be able to do something in time to save his home. It would take time and more people like him to help us build a coalition. I watched as the hopefulness in his eyes drained away. With a tinge of resignation, he agreed to do whatever he could to help out. Before we finished our coffee, I worked up the courage to ask him the question that had failed so many times before: "Carlos, who else in your neighborhood should I be talking to about this?" He looked around the diner first, checking to make sure nobody was within earshot, and then leaned in to answer me in a hushed tone: "Everybody, Elan. Everybody."

One cup of coffee, one unrushed conversation, revealed to me what I'd failed to catch in dozens of other meetings. It was Carlos who knew what this community needed, not me. It was the mess he found himself in, the secret that he feared would make him untrustworthy in my eyes, that opened up the real work that needed to be done. Maribeth was right; I needed to put myself in the way of many of these conversations each week. I needed to let almost everything else go so I could be fully present and listen with real care to what Carlos knew about this community and I did not. I learned that day—not for the first time or the last—that trusting what other people see in the world is as essential as trusting what I can see with my own eyes.

Inspired Restlessness

Restlessness, the stirring that signals something is not right, is the root of every great religious movement. Many of the world's religions were founded by one restless soul who heard a higher power's call to leave behind the world that they were born into. It was that restlessness that caused Abraham (Gen 12:1; then known as Avram) to leave his father's homeland, Jesus to seek wisdom outside his parents' traditional home (Luke 2:49–50), the Buddha to start his journey to enlightenment.

Restlessness moves us beyond the realm of faith traditions too. We see the restlessness of the oppressed in every uprising for justice—in the Arab Spring, in the anti-mandatory-hijab movement in Iran, in multiple iterations of the civil rights movement in the United States. Restlessness drives job changes and new career directions. It moves people to seek new places, to learn new skills, to walk away from destructive relationships. All chosen change—systemic, institutional, even personal—is rooted in restlessness.

Reading our own restlessness is a skill of leadership. Intuitive leaders trust their gut. Faith-minded leaders are practiced at listening to the voice of a spirit beyond their own. We know our restlessness is a sign that we are being called to make a turn, to move in another direction. But who else's restlessness matters? Whose intolerance for things as they are now ought to compel us toward action? Who else might bear the new word of God that resonates with our own agitation?

Those impulses are everywhere. The most restless among us are rarely our most compliant followers. They're not the ones who show up early and leave late, who fill the front-row pews, whose hands shoot up when volunteers are sought. They don't darken your doorway for earnest conversation on Tuesday afternoons, or chair your education committee, or come asking how they can help. No, the restless among us are all too often no longer among us. They're the ones who left the community years ago after several frustrating attempts to initiate change. And if they're still hanging around, they sit in the last row. Sometimes they lean against the back wall of the sanctuary, poised to leave at a moment's notice. Restlessness tends to bubble up from the margins: the back of the room, the sidelines of our communities, the sometimes-but-not-always participants. Maybe you even recognize in these dissatisfied folks a dim reflection of your own discontent.

Discovering restlessness, trusting the voices that bring it to you, might be the most sacred, urgent task of these days. For once those who experience it are truly heard, the potential for them to point our communities toward change is immense.

Experience, Not Expertise: Sara Luria's Story

A first meeting with the rabbi and entrepreneur Sara Luria is striking: she is genuinely happy to meet you. Many faith leaders train themselves to hold a smile for hours on end, to learn people's names with mnemonic devices, to look folks in the eye when speaking to them. But Luria's friendliness is not an engagement tactic, or a calculated method of memorizing your name, or a welcoming technique she picked up at some professional development conference. For her, it's because she has recognized something beloved in you. Luria has that rare capacity to light up the people around her, not just the room.

From her formative adolescent years, Luria has shaped her whole leadership journey around doing just that—lifting up others in love, in hope, and in power. And for her, it all starts with trust. "When I was in high school, I was a 'good girl' who secretly rebelled. And I always felt like the adults talked down to us, rather than seeking our input to shape our educational experiences. What did we know? There were just so many times where I wondered: 'Why aren't we being trusted? We know how this school impacts students. We are the students. Why don't they trust us with that?'"[7] Luria's teenage logic was straightforward. What could be more trustworthy than the students' lived experiences? If those in power would just trust the students to help shape their own learning, to tell the adults what they needed and wanted to learn, then everyone would win. The teachers could teach materials that resonated, and students would in turn pay more attention because they would be part owners in their education.

All the way through high school and college, Luria continued to wonder about how people in positions of power might do better if they trusted the people they served. After college, her first job was with a Jewish, faith-based community organizing fellowship called JOIN for Justice. "When I was in the JOIN Fellowship," she says, "I was taught this line: 'The people closest to the problem are the experts.' And that rang so true for me."[8]

Community organizing taught Luria that in every community there are countless experts whose wisdom is just waiting to be sought out. Not the ones who sought PhDs or went through years of professional training to become experts. No, it's the ones with real lived experience. Parenting experts who juggle multiple children and myriad responsibilities. Homelessness experts who have grown skilled at surviving without reliable and permanent shelter. Loneliness experts who have discovered tools for negotiating their isolated lives. Scriptures may hold textual wisdom to guide us through each of these life states, but she wondered: How much more inspiring would Scripture's words be if they were paired with the experience-tested wisdom of a divinely made person from your neighborhood?

A Doula for the Soul

At the same time she was attending rabbinical school, the effervescent Luria also began coursework to become a doula, a professional trained to support and guide mothers through labor and childbirth. She was intentional about pursuing these tracks simultaneously; each brought a profound experience of being formed as a new identity—mother, rabbi. Examining each of these identities closely, she suspected, might allow them to inform each other.

> I became a doula, and it was extraordinarily impactful on my rabbinate, which I was not expecting. The doula's job is not medical; it's support—emotional, spiritual, and physical. When you walk into the training to become a doula, they say: "You've self-selected to be someone who supports a laboring person through a really, really intense transition. You already know everything you need to know about doing this. We are going to give you some extra skills, but the fact that you've already self-selected to be here means you are the right person to be here."
>
> And I just thought, "Wow." Almost every other situation I've ever walked into where I was learning something, I got the impression that the teachers thought I didn't know

anything, and they were going to fill me up with knowledge. And it never rang true to me. I always felt, "But I know so much." I know things in my body, I know things in my heart. I have experience. I have life experience, and that gives me expertise.

This doula training was just the opposite. I was so enlightened by it. I thought, that's how we should do everything. All our teaching should be turned on its head. We should say to the people who walk in the room, "I trust you and I believe in you. I know you have certain expertise and certain experience in various things. And I want to learn, I want you to change my life."[9]

When Luria graduated from rabbinical school and was ordained, she knew in her heart that the traditional model of pulpit leadership wasn't for her. She had watched friends take on those roles. She'd watched them shape themselves around the expectations of sage-on-the-stage leadership. Luria knew herself well enough to be sure that her calling was to be a guide on the side. Or, perhaps more precisely, a midwife in the middle. She says, "My job is to be a catalyst for harnessing the wisdom of the folks in the room. My job is to facilitate a way for *other* people to feel powerful in who they are, and what they know, and what they can share."[10]

Luria had a clear vision for the kind of leadership she was called to. Now she just had to create the organization she would lead.

ImmerseNYC

In Jewish life, there are countless rituals that mark time and make meaning, from lighting the Sabbath candles, to saying a prayer before meals, to offering an intimate blessing to one's children every Friday night. But few rituals have become more misunderstood and siloed than immersing in the *mikveh*, a ritual bath first described in Leviticus as a rite that confers a meticulous level of purity. Over a number of centuries, *mikveh* evolved. Concerns about ritual purity seemed to many Jews outdated relics of a time long past; *mikveh* became a ritual practiced almost exclusively in Orthodox settings.

In recent years, however, a number of efforts have been made to expand the use of *mikveh* outside Orthodox circles and beyond the ancient occasions of Levitical purity. Sara Luria was one of the earliest pioneers in this effort to expand access to *mikveh*. But she knew that widening that doorway wouldn't happen if she just tried to pry it open herself. She needed to empower a circle of women to take ownership over their ritual lives and inspire them to support others to do so too.

Luria founded ImmerseNYC with a clear-eyed vision: the *mikveh* could become a place where people from all walks of Jewish life could mark time—celebrations, losses, and everything in between—by engaging in this ancient, embodied ritual that might leave them feeling renewed and restored in body, mind, and spirit.

ImmerseNYC was not an overnight success. Luria's vision met resistance from some Orthodox leaders, doubt from potential funders, and cynicism from colleagues who couldn't really see the world the way she saw it. Luria wrote countless grant proposals during those early years; she can recite verbatim the canned language of rejection letters. She applied to fellowships and incubators, pitched to every donor willing to hear her out, and kept on grinding until, eventually, the tides slowly began to turn. A few years in, she was drawing a modest salary, had established key partnerships with *mikvehs* throughout New York City, and recruited a dedicated group of volunteer leaders to support ImmerseNYC's growth.

Once the organization was finally on solid ground, its leader also began to attract attention. Luria regularly fielded invitations to speak about her accomplishments in building a successful venture. News outlets, philanthropic foundations, and thought leaders wanted to learn from her success, and they invited her to use their channels to promote herself. Panels at the Aspen Institute Ideas Festival, keynotes at major religion conferences, magazine profiles, podcast appearances—all of these platforms invited Luria into the spotlight. It was a privilege her success had earned.

But self-promotion was not Luria's way. No matter how she was prompted by the interviewer or host, she turned attention toward the powerful stories of her "*mikveh* guides"—the volunteers she had trained to facilitate the ancient, intimate ritual. In Luria's eyes, these were the heroes of the story. These were women who had dared to reimagine an ancient, immovable relic of their tradition. Luria had invited them to step into power she knew they already held. She had said to them, early on, "I want you to change my life," and they had agreed. These were the people, Luria says, who were most responsible for ImmerseNYC's success.

> What I had always been taught about training volunteers to facilitate ritual is that they needed to know a lot about the ritual and the history of the ritual and the technicalities of the ritual, and all that stuff. But I had this feeling that the people who showed up to stand with someone who was in this life transition already had everything they needed. My job was to give them permission to enact the ritual and to say to them, "I trust you, I believe in you. I know you have everything within you."[11]

Wisdom in the Room

As ImmerseNYC continued to grow, so did Luria's conviction that her larger Jewish community needed a different model of organizational leadership, one formed not by organizational theory but by the community's theology. Theologies are multiple, of course, even within a single faith tradition. The soul of our organizations is slanted by our choice of *which* theology we use to guide their leadership. Are we turning to the bearded man in the sky for inspiration? Or to a loving Creator who sought to instill divinity in each of God's creatures? "It wasn't my idea that we are beloved by God. It's not like, 'Oh, Rabbi Sara has this weird theology.' That belovedness is in the Song of Songs. But even more so it's in our breath. God's breath being within us, being reflections of God. How can we build communal spaces that are like *that*?"[12]

In many of the panel discussions and interviews Luria spoke in during the years she promoted ImmerseNYC, someone would ask a question about the technical aspects of building a successful startup. What's your business model? How did you scale so quickly? What's your secret? Luria never missed an opportunity to circle back to theology. If you truly believe that everyone is beloved in the eyes of God, she would say, then everything you do as you're building your organization should be a reflection of that core belief. It should inform how you greet newcomers when they show up to an event. It should come through on your home page as clear as day. And, most importantly, it should dictate how you treat the people around you, with no exceptions. That doesn't just mean treating them kindly; that's just the baseline. It means trusting them even when there's some risk involved. It means holding them accountable, even if that means having an uncomfortable conversation, so long as it's rooted in love. "The empire wants us to think that we're just always lacking," she says. "Someone always knows more than us, and it's a competition, and you're at the bottom, and you just need more and more and more. But to me, leadership is about harnessing the wisdom in rooms of people. My job as the leader is to be a catalyst for that wisdom to appear. What I can do is help other people feel powerful in who they are, and what they know, and what they can share. That's my job."[13]

Expertise or Experience?

ImmerseNYC has inspired a growing network of similar projects around the country. As the organization grew, it became clear to Luria that her calling, too, had evolved. Her next project was Beloved Garden, a national network to support the leaders of new Jewish communities of spirituality and practice, communities founded on the simple theological conviction that every person is beloved, trusted, loved, empowered.

It was another ambitious vision. And again, Luria ran into layers of resistance. It's one thing to build a local organization with a modest budget around the notion of belovedness; it's entirely another to build a national network of faith leaders who have already demonstrated enough initiative to start a new faith community. Some of Luria's supporters and board members advised her to stabilize the organization before she reached out to form a first cohort. They urged her to build infrastructure and brand first, secure funding, wrap up the website, finalize the training curriculum. "Building a national network isn't like building a plane mid-flight," they warned her. She pushed back. If the Beloved Garden was going to embody her theology of belovedness, it would have to remain pliable. It needed a vision gathered not just from its founder but from everyone who would become a part of it.

Luria was clear: she would not be the "expert" in this organization. Her job would not be to pour wisdom into cohorts of emerging leaders. She had plenty of hard-won expertise under her belt, but everybody else in the room would have some experience too. She wanted them to share it. "Once you feel like you're an expert, you forget what it was like to not have had a lot of experience. You lose the sense of being connected. You get so high up there in the organizational structure that you forget what it was like to be down at the bottom of the pyramid. I want to say to leaders, 'Let's just stay in it with the people. Let's just stay in it.'"[14]

Beloved Garden grew, but not without struggles. There were administrative headaches; as it turns out, offering fiscal sponsorship to dozens of organizations while your organization is still in start-up mode is complicated. There were fundraising challenges, foundations that loved the mission and wanted to support the good work but decided to wait until the model proved sustainable before making an investment. There were leadership disappointments; not every person with whom Luria tried to share power stepped into it wholeheartedly. Luria sees these growing pains as simply part of the process of believing in and reminding folks of their belovedness. She says,

> The way my coach puts it, even if you made mistakes and you forgot to apologize, even if you get a bad haircut, even if you really suck at playing the tuba, or you were scared, whatever it is, you're loved just the same. And you're worthy of love, just the same. No behavior can take that away. And even if people just believe it for half a second, or even if they roll their eyes at us, it will suddenly hit them on a random Tuesday morning that they're beloved by God, that they are worthy of love. That's good. That's a start.[15]

▲

Trust—Just Try It On:
Moses's Story

Moses's first and most vivid model of what a leader looks like was Pharaoh. It was a brittle command-and-control image, left in splinters amid the rubble of the first stone tablets. But until that moment of shattering, Moses's understanding of his call to leadership had been filtered through a vision Moses had watched work efficiently in Pharaoh's empire. It still made sense to him: God had singled Moses out among the entire nation; he was the chosen one among an entire chosen people. So when their life in community required governing systems and a judge to resolve disputes among the people, Moses did what any prince raised by the empire would have done: he climbed up to the top of the pyramid and got to work.

And work he did. On his first day as a judge, "Moses sat as magistrate among the people, while the people stood about

Moses from morning until evening" (Exod 18:13, The Contemporary Torah, JPS, 2006). The text does not tell us of the accuracy or efficacy of Moses's judgments, or of the people's confidence in his discretion. But the people stood patiently and passively for the entire day while he worked through his caseload, one by one.

Yitro is the priest of Midian.[16] He's also Moses's father-in-law, which might make him one of the only people in the community who isn't afraid to challenge Moses, to ask him hard questions. Yitro watches the scene of people standing around all day waiting for their turn to talk, and then he asks Moses, "What is this thing that you are doing to the people? Why do you act alone, while all the people stand about you from morning until evening?" (Exod 18:14). Moses's reply signals he has no idea what Yitro is talking about. He hasn't even noticed that his tight grip on arbitration authority means that every Thursday, all the other work in the camp stops while people wait for him to rule on their neighborhood frictions. Moses answers directly, but a little obtusely, "It is because the people come to me to inquire of God. When they have a dispute, it comes before me, and I decide between one party and another, and I make known the laws and teachings of God" (Exod 18:15–16).

Yitro is wise. He can see that Moses's intention is to be conscientious, that he is taking seriously his call to leadership of this people who, it seems, regularly get caught up in their own rabblement. Moses's heart is in the right place. His strategy is not. Yitro chides him for trying to do it all himself. "The thing you are doing is not right; you will surely wear yourself out, and these people as well. For the task is too heavy for you; you cannot do it alone" (Exod 18:17–19).

Yitro has practical advice:

> *Now listen to me. I will give you counsel, and God be with you!*
> *You represent the people before God: you bring the disputes*
> *before God, and enjoin upon them the laws and the teachings,*

and make known to them the way they are to go and the practices they are to follow.

You shall also seek out, from among all the people, capable individuals who fear God—trustworthy ones who spurn ill-gotten gain. Set these over them as chiefs of thousands, hundreds, fifties, and tens, and let them judge the people at all times. Have them bring every major dispute to you, but let them decide every minor dispute themselves. Make it easier for yourself by letting them share the burden with you.

If you do this—and God so commands you—you will be able to bear up; and all these people too will go home unwearied. (Exod 18:19–23)

In the long tradition of prophets everywhere, Yitro sees something Moses cannot. The view from the top of the pyramid is limited; the perspective of those at the bottom is too distant to take in. Yitro's advice to Moses seems laughably simple: Step one: You teach the Torah; that's what you know best. Step two: Find trustworthy people. Step three: Let them lead. Yitro's message to Moses is: You don't have to do everything. You *can't* do everything. And if you try, you will cause more lasting harm than you can imagine.

How do we know who is trustworthy and who isn't? How do we know who will step up when called on, who will hold the organization's mission and honor its values the way we do ourselves? How do we know who will merit our confidence when we take the personal and professional risk of sharing the power that has been entrusted to us? The truth is: we don't know. It wouldn't be a risk if it were a sure thing.

In the words of the theologian and activist adrienne maree brown, "Trust the people. If you trust them, they become trustworthy."[17] Like all faith, entrusting critical responsibilities to others requires a step forward without a clear view of the ground ahead. The more we trust our people, the further we move away from the empire. It is an imperative to us, a necessary step on the way to the promise ahead.

Notes

1   Teresa Mitrovic, *The Currency of Connection: How Trust Transforms Life, Relationships, and Work* (London: New Generation, 2020), 36.

2   Stephen M. Covey, *Trust and Inspire : How Truly Great Leaders Unleash Greatness in Others* (New York: Simon & Schuster, 2022), 48.

3   Paul Zak, *The Moral Molecule*, quoted in Mitrovic, *Currency of Connection*, 38.

4   Quoted in Mitrovic, *Currency of Connection*, 33.

5   Founded in 1940, the Industrial Areas Foundation quickly grew into a national community-organizing network and has driven some of the most lasting and powerful social and political changes in the decades since.

6   I didn't discover the winding canyon roads—a formerly well-kept secret shortcut for LA commuters and an outright joy to drive with a stick shift—until my time as an organizer was almost over.

7   Sara Luria, interview, August 25, 2022.

8   Luria, interview.

9   Luria, interview.

10 Luria, interview.

11 Luria, interview.

12 Luria, interview.

13 Luria, interview.

14 Luria, interview.

15 Luria, interview.

16 In Anglicized translations, Jethro.

17 adrienne maree brown, *Emergent Strategy* (repr., Chico, CA: AK Press, 2017), 214.

CHAPTER EIGHT

Leadership in the Wilderness

Power Struggles: Kathi's Story

I had been the lead pastor at my church for more than four years when the team of senior staff members ran into a logjam in our communications with each other. Team members were routinely working separately, steering away from opportunities for collaboration that would have deepened the effectiveness of our ministries. We were misunderstanding, and consequently resenting, one another's intentions and motives.

So one day at a team meeting, I proposed a new practice. I'd designed it carefully; I was sure it would help us move toward more collaborative and less siloed ministries and responsibilities. Every week, I proposed, each team member would be paired with another. Throughout the week we'd all spend one hour observing our partner's work and then a little more time together to talk about our observations and (I hoped) new appreciation for each other's ministry responsibilities. It seemed to me like a perfect plan: a low investment of time and a measurable return on that investment in mutual respect and understanding of one another's work. No-brainer, I thought. I introduced the idea close to the end of our regular staff meeting, thinking it would be a quick agenda item.

I was totally unprepared for the litany of objections that came as readily as a scripted call-and-response. "I can't spare that kind of time." "I don't see why this is important." "This feels like too much pressure." "I don't need to know that much detail about my colleagues' work."

I was stunned. I tried to listen as nondefensively as I could. As we closed the meeting, I said I would think about their objections and whether the project could be adjusted to meet them.

Afterward, a few members of the team expressed surprise that I'd let the discussion get away from me and that I'd allowed their colleagues to refuse to do what the senior pastor asked. I began to ask myself similar questions. Even if they had reservations, why would staff members not just defer to the authority of my position? Should I have insisted that everyone just do what I was telling them to do?

And then perhaps the most telling question, with the most consequential answer: Am I the only one who feels charged with thinking about the good of the whole organization? Can I trust others to act beyond their personal agendas and preferences?

We never did that exercise; it felt to me not worth the battle. But I've thought a lot about that moment. Does empowering other people include empowering their resistance to my leadership?

We Are Meant to Be Moving

Human beings like order and stability. Being able to predict what will come next makes us feel confident about how we move forward in the world. In fact, it could fairly be said that this is one of the goals of education: to learn to see historical and physical patterns, laws of nature and human behavior, well enough that we know what is coming next. The idea that a predictable order is God's intention for the earth is also embedded deep in our theology. The creation story in Genesis is a story of God stilling the chaos that reigned before earth and water were separated into their proper places, until species were divided, until creatures had their names.

And yet, there is another persistent pattern in the biblical narrative, not to be ignored. God seems constantly eager to disrupt the patterns and rules of human convention, the foundations of institutional life. Just when we think we have figured out what God intended for us and we set our feet in bedrock, God uproots us. "Get up and go" was the word of God to Abraham, Jacob, and Moses, to Joseph and Mary when a king's decree threatened their child's safety. When the Israelites structured their life around intricate rituals they thought were incumbent on them, God countered, "Your new moons and fixed seasons fill Me with loathing; they have become a burden to Me. I cannot endure them" (Isa 1:14; Amos 5:21).

The Christian Gospels are full of stories in which Jesus challenges the religious structures of his own tradition: Jewish Sabbath practices, their system of temple sacrifices, the purity codes that had always marked the Israelites as the people of God.

We humans can get stuck in the search for solid ground beneath our feet, encased in the plaster of a pyramid that protects us from the elements. The drift into rigidity, an inability to respond to a summons to movement, happens around our good intentions, often without our even noticing. Immobility often looks to us like faithfulness—to a tradition or a way of life that was never intended to be fixed forever.

The *wilderness* is a metaphor for the dislocation and precariousness we experience when our familiar patterns of predictability and certainty are disrupted. The biblical story suggests that God regularly drives even favored people into the wilderness when something important is about to change: the Israelites on the way out of slavery, John the Baptist on the way to justice work, Jesus on the cusp of a life of self-sacrifice. The wilderness is always full of conflict and temptation. The wilderness is where we are destabilized until something cracks, opening us to rethinking what we thought we knew for sure. It's where we realize we need something we have not yet possessed or even discovered. The wilderness is where we learn that curiosity and humility are our most important tools for venturing, and for leading, into God's unpredictable future.

Living Liturgy: De'Amon Harges's Story

These are the names De'Amon Harges has given his neighbors: Gift Finder. Neighborhood Healer. Cultivator of Joy. Minister of Propaganda. Lady of Justice and Humanity. These are not your run-of-the-mill church job titles. But then again, De'Amon Harges is not a run-of-the-mill leader.

Harges, too, has been known by a number of names and titles over the years. From his artist name, Parradoux,[1] to his title of social banker in his community, to the label he's most commonly known by—the Roving Listener—De'Amon travels through the world known by many names. And he does so on, and with, purpose. He says, "The power of naming is everything. We learn that in our spiritual practices. I'm an identifier, a person that looks for people's gifts, in ways that fit their types. So the names I use, and the ones I offer to others, they're really tied into our being, and it gives us the power to name our own value instead of letting the empire do it for us."[2]

These days, Harges travels all over the world looking for and activating those gifts in others. But it wasn't always this way. Growing up in South Bend, Indiana, with a deep commitment to putting down local roots, he was already a young adult by the time he first boarded a plane. "My mom used to say to me, 'I think you're going to be traveling the world.' Now, I didn't travel until I turned twenty; I think it was my first trip on a plane. But all the time my mom would say, 'Well, De'Amon, you're going to be the guy that gets on the trains and train-hops all over.' So I came back to tell my mother, 'Hey, we created this job title, the Roving Listener.' And she said, 'That is you.'"[3]

Harges sees the world in ways that most folks do not. He is remarkably observant, and he asks questions that take you to all kinds of unexpected places. He comes across like a faithful student of the world, curious through and through. It is precisely that curiosity that helps him see abundance where others see deficits, discover gifts where others might not even bother looking, and activate those gifts in transformative ways.

Twenty years into his life in Indianapolis, Harges's most valuable journeys now are the ones he takes around the neighborhood surrounding Broadway United Methodist Church, where he has served in a number of roles over the years. These four-block walks, long a staple of his service in the community, are how he widens his aperture of the world and the people around him. They are his compass for navigating the wilderness of the moment and encountering God in all places. As recounted by his colleague, Reverend Michael Mather, Harges never emerges from those walks empty-handed:

> He started walking the four blocks from his home to Broadway to see me several times a week. He always brought a story about someone he met along the walk . . . about the man who sat on his porch playing chess and how young people gathered around and talked with him and challenged him to a game . . . about the young men who stood on street corners, talking and keeping an eye on things in the neighborhood. He learned who the artists were, and who the teachers were, and who the entrepreneurs were.[4]

Living Liturgy

In stark contrast to the recruitment efforts of many other ministry professionals who scour their neighborhoods for potential members, Harges didn't take these walks so that he could convince folks to come to church. In fact, just the opposite. His goal was for his colleagues and parishioners to mold the church around the stories of the people who lived in the neighborhood.

He wanted to ensure that the transcendent experience of the church—witness, care, grace—would move outward, into the neighborhood, no longer locked inside its walls. He didn't want those folks to become more like the church; he wanted the church to become more like them.

And he knew he couldn't do it alone; as many nicknames as he had adopted, he was still just one person, and Broadway was just one church. A hub-and-spoke model of community building would never work. It's not how Harges moves through the world. He treats each story as if it were Scripture, with reverence, care, and responsibility. The stories—and the people who share them—become a sort of living liturgy throughout the neighborhood. The more that folks share those stories, the more they come to witness the gifts that underscore each of them, and the more willing they are to contribute those gifts to the transformation of the neighborhood.

Every time he walked those blocks, Harges found new walking partners, new stories to share, and new connections to make. He also began to see that many of the gifts these folks had to share matched beautifully with the needs he was also hearing. "People know you for the powers you bring, but when you come in, your job is to listen. They already had the answers to things. I practiced asking questions that would highlight or bear witness to things that people didn't always see for themselves."[5]

God Is Already Here

In neighborhoods like the one around Broadway United Methodist Church, Harges knows, the focus tends to be on what is lacking. What the problems are. Where the scarcity is most acutely experienced. He's not naive; the lack is real, as are the problems and the scarcity. But by drawing attention to the places where solutions are already in place, where abundance is truly felt, where gifts are waiting to be brought to bear, Harges has helped to advance what he believes to be God's dream for the lives of those in the community. For Harges, his work isn't about inviting God into the neighborhood; it's about underscoring that God is already there. "What is the role of the social system, the church, if we cannot see, if we cannot touch, if we cannot make what was once invisible, visible?"[6]

But It's Complicated

Harges's work, though largely fruitful over its first two decades, has not been without significant challenges. Bringing church into the neighborhood introduces complicated power dynamics, and there are times when they turn into power struggles. Just getting people to answer the door when he rings the bell can sometimes be an obstacle. When he began to speak for the church, that obstacle sometimes looked more like a wall. Mather says,

> When De'Amon began his work, he discovered something pretty quickly. Before starting the job, he had knocked on doors as a neighbor, and people had talked with him easily, welcoming him into their homes. But when he began this new job by introducing himself as a representative of the church and the development corporation, people weren't very welcoming to him. So he went back to what worked. People didn't trust institutions, but they trusted neighbors.[7]

Harges's consciousness about that distinction—between maintaining an institution and acting as a neighbor—presents a constant tension, a theme in his organizing work. He checks in regularly with himself, his colleagues, and the neighbors that Broadway United Methodist Church serves to ensure that he is showing up in the world as a neighbor first. He acts on behalf of the institution, but every day he is attentive to all that representation brings. The creep of institutional concerns is constant; Harges is vigilant about privileging people over programs, stories over structure.

Once he does get invited in by his neighbors, the Roving Listener keenly appreciates the immense responsibility that comes with that opening. It takes time—sometimes a huge investment of it—to build the kind of relationship that merits his entrustment with something so precious as a person's story. That trust is fragile. What he does with those stories matters a great deal. Each story shared with him puts a claim on Harges's heart. As he mines that story for the gift hidden in its teller and carries that gift into the light, another threshold is raised in Harges's commitment to bear witness. "You have to make a commitment to figuring out how the gifts you've discovered can be utilized, and how you celebrate that not just with each other, but with the world."[8]

Receiving people's stories and lifting up the gifts of those around him is just the beginning of Harges's work. Inviting action out of those stories, and generosity out of those gifts, is the next step. Sometimes it's the hardest. Taking his organizing energy to other churches, Harges has discovered that not every congregation wants to imagine the future, let alone contribute their efforts into bringing it about. "Some of the churches I've been working with have had a hard time thinking about their future because they've been stuck in nostalgia from the past. It stops them from thinking about what could yet become."[9]

Not everyone in our communities is ready to make change. Some are quite happy with the world as it is. Others are willing to live in an unjust world out of fear of the unknown. Still others are holding onto an idealized version of the past. For all the good that change might promise, the grip of the way things used to be can be even more compelling.

In fact, sometimes the folks who resist change are the ones who hold the most power in their communities. They may be elected officials, congregation members with prominent titles, or other folks coming in from outside the neighborhood. Whoever they are, Harges is aware of the potential for power imbalances in his work. Sometimes there is a suspicion by neighborhood folks that the church is only out there to recruit, not to serve. Other times, there are churches that use their financial or political influence to make changes in the neighborhood without pausing for buy-in from those who actually live in it. Getting ahead of these potentially disruptive power plays is critical to building trust from the outset and relationships for the long run.

After some experiences in which those very imbalances caused setbacks, Harges created a new rule, one that leveled the playing field and invited the neighbors to speak up with confidence and safety. "And the rule was that when we had these gatherings, people in power couldn't talk. They had to listen. They could ask certain questions, but they had to be intent on discovering what was invisible, until it became visible."[10]

The work of raising into visibility and power the stories and gifts of people often not seen by our congregations requires humility, curiosity, and patience. These are not passive values; they're disciplines. They require daily practice, sometimes wrestling with objections, habits, and even institutional interests. They demand of leaders a willingness to spend time on work that does not translate immediately into productivity measurements. They tolerate, even welcome, edges that look messy and unformed.

As challenging as this work has been, it is deeply fulfilling for Harges. It has also made a profound impact on his church and the community surrounding it. Entering a third decade of this work in the same neighborhood has invited him to reflect on successes and failures and to adapt his work. There are countless ways for Harges to keep growing into the title "Roving Listener." The actual work will no doubt keep changing. "I remember when I first started roving listening. I was doing it by myself. And I went through this whole thing thinking you have to be just one thing, like a hub to everybody's spokes. And it's just not the way. Stars don't operate like that. And planets? We can't even fully comprehend how they operate, but they do. Each in their own way, they do. Heaven's a witness."[11]

Leaps of Faith: Father Richard Springer's Story

It wasn't the easiest job on the table for Father Richard Springer to consider back in 2018, when he was discerning his next role. Nor was it the most prominent. But when the opportunity arose to serve as rector of St. George-in-the-East, a three-hundred-year-old Anglican church in London, he knew this was an offer he could not refuse. "Firstly, it's God, isn't it? It's a belief that your life really isn't your own. You are here for a time, all that stuff that is easy to say and harder to live out. But I do believe that my decisions are attempts at trying to understand God's will. And so I have to put my trust in that."[12]

Indeed, Springer is a man of broad and abiding faith—in God and in people. Like Harges, he was shaped by the power of neighborhoods from a very young age, watching the ways that his father, a Pentecostal pastor, activated the passions of those around him. "He knew everybody in the street. And I grew up in that kind of environment where the pastor was someone who was part of the community. I think I was essentially formed that way as a Christian."[13]

Inspired by his father's way in the world, Springer spent the early part of his career serving communities in similar ways. He worked with children and families, as part of a small charity in a housing estate,[14] in social policy work, and as a community organizer. Whenever he began working in a new location, he would spend considerable time and effort rooting himself in the local community so he could serve the people in more deep, sustainable, and impactful ways.

Springer had a friend, an Anglican priest named Angus Ritchie, whom he respected immensely and who had successfully introduced community organizing into the church he led. "He (Ritchie) had this vision of community organizing and developing a congregation with the poorest and most marginalized at the heart of it. Not serving those people, but those people indeed revealing God to everybody, including themselves and the community. I was drawn by that vision."[15]

This was the vision that led Springer into ministry from the very beginning. But his path was unusual. "I became the assistant priest with a view to becoming the rector. That's not the normal route to becoming rector. But we swapped. He [Ritchie] is now the assistant priest, and I am the rector. Which is very unusual. It was possible because he has a truly healthy and uncommon awareness of ego. It was always the plan, but it's very unusual actually to take that route."[16] Springer was confident this was the work that God wanted him to do. He would stand on the shoulders of a colleague who led with generosity and not ego. He was convinced that everything he had learned about community empowerment could weave a deep connection between the neighborhood and the church. It was enough to suggest that this would not be a typical church job.

But it would require another one of those proverbial leaps of faith. Springer knew a lot about communities. His faith found a home in the church, but the connection was not obvious. Could a church actually adapt its institutional focus enough to transform from the outside in, giving voice and power to those in its neighborhood who had never been fully welcomed before? Would it be too disruptive to make such a radical shift?

Springer became an assistant priest in 2016, and rector of his urban congregation in 2018. At the core of the challenge were questions of power. The church, and Springer himself, would have to wrestle consciously with the reality of their presence in the community. Sharing the power that comes with institutional status is a simple concept on paper but much more complicated in practice.

Power Is Not Zero Sum

There are many important rituals for faith-based leaders who engage in community organizing. There are the coffee-fueled one-to-one meetings, where practices of appreciative inquiry often lead to breakthrough revelations. There are the inspirational sermons, designed to ignite a passion for systems change among parishioners. Then there are the town-hall meetings, where storytelling becomes the driver of the organizing vehicle, supplanting both information and expertise.

As important as these practices are, they only work when institutional leaders are conscious of the workings of power: the power of the political systems they seek to change, the power of the new leaders they're cultivating, and, most importantly, their own power, whether they're sitting at a coffee shop or preaching from the pulpit. Springer has a particularly nuanced view of how power works in his context.

> One thing that's crucial to understand is that power is not a zero-sum game.[17] When I invite others to lead, I'm not giving away my power as a leader of my church. I am powerful in my church and I'm okay with that. And your experience as a member of this church is to learn to recognize that you too can be powerful and use that power appropriately—not to have power over people, but to build power with people. But I don't have more power than you, such that I need to give some of my power to you. That's not how it works. I'm not giving you my power. It belongs to me. And your power belongs to you.[18]

Leadership of the Unlikeliest

To an Anglican priest in a formal, historic institution like St. George-in-the-East, the concept of shared power does not come naturally. There is one, and only one, rector. Clergy and the congregation alike expect that the rector will hold the community's religious authority. The paradox is that to effectively engage a community in organizing, that very same rector, who holds a singular and clearly established role as *the* leader, must step out of that spotlight. Leaving some vacancy is critical to creating space for new leaders to emerge. It is a delicate dance, this move toward a finely tuned balance of power. As the steps have become more familiar, Springer has been delighted to witness the kinds of folks who have stepped onto the dance floor with him.

> You don't want the leader of your church to be left with no power because he's given it or she's given it all away. That's no good. I think crucially in any faith institution we learn about power-sharing leadership from God. Sharing does not reduce God's power. Instead it enables others to operate in power—particularly those who are least likely or indeed completely unlikely to hold power. Often, they are the ones who exercise it well and in fact change things for the better, because their position of unlikeliness enables them to see the world differently.[19]

Springer is persistent about inviting unlikely persons to act as leaders, to sample holding their own power. He encourages folks from the margins to step right into the center—at meetings, in worship, and in other kinds of gatherings. He watches with delight how their presence and perspectives bring fresh thoughts into the experience for everyone. When one of those new leaders shares a story or simply shows up, it expands the worldview of everyone in the room. Witnessing this surprising demonstration prompts the community to see the world differently. A wider lens has expanded the church's vision in myriad ways, from programmatic to political, relational to ritual. Some of those impacts are difficult to measure. Perhaps they're not even noticeable at first glance. But over time, growth often shows up in measurable ways too.

Before it began the community-organizing approach that Springer has made the church's hallmark, the congregation was small, like many aging urban churches. Many of its attendees drove from outside the local neighborhood to attend. But in the years just before the pandemic, the organizing work brought more and more people into the building. "By the time Covid came in 2020, we witnessed an exponential growth of people worshiping regularly, with a lot more people from the neighborhood. They weren't all coming regularly on Sundays, but they were part of activities throughout the week. So we were enjoying a much, much bigger community."

For Springer, the measurement that mattered was not about increased attendance; the kind of faith he calls people to practice is not a spectator sport. But as more and more folks stepped into the halls of St. George-in-the-East, what they encountered was not just a magnificent building with echoing acoustics in the sanctuary. They noticed that every voice immediately joined the harmony of this growing community. Each person who entered received a meaningful invitation to shape the future of what would take place inside that building, what the community as a whole would stand for, and whom they would stand with.

Roots in a Restless Neighborhood

There are always challenges in leading a community through change. The stakes multiply when the composition of the community is also shifting. Bringing in new members while you are honoring the existing ones can be complicated. St. George-in-the-East felt the tension intensely as the church's leaders looked to develop alignment across generations, cultures, and a variety of lived experiences. Springer says,

> This is something I'm challenged by right now. We're at that stage where people are coming because they've heard St. George-in-the East is an interesting church, but they're not necessarily local, and they're not necessarily fully bought into what we're doing. They're not exactly tourists, but mostly they're coming because they're curious. How do

we explain power sharing to people who aren't rooted in the neighborhood?

We want to put the poorest and the unlikeliest at the heart of the church, but God is there for the richest and the middle classes as well. The challenge to those people isn't to give away their money or to volunteer half the week; that's not the solution. The solution is to figure out how to become rooted in a neighborhood.[20]

Almost a decade in, Springer's roots now run deep in the community. He draws strength and inspiration from soil both inside and outside the church. But he's come to see that his experiences are his alone; his perspective isn't universal. Inviting others—newcomers and long-tenured members both—to put down roots requires the long, patient work of planting and watching something grow on its own. His leadership is an exercise in space making, storytelling, and welcoming surprises along the way.

There is a woman in our congregation who lived without a home for ten years and who is now homed and who is part of our homelessness ministry. And she is constantly challenging the congregation. At one stage she said, "We're doing this homelessness work, but there's no invitation to homeless people to worship—as if they either don't need it or don't have a belief in God. How about if we start serving breakfast before the Mass on Sunday morning?"[21]

For years, church members had interacted with a few of the unhoused people living near the church. They'd given out money and food, talked with their homeless neighbors, and connected them to support services. But until this woman spoke, the church had never seriously contemplated weaving those neighbors into the fabric of the worshiping congregation. It was a blind spot, and this woman was pointing to it, saying, "I see something you don't." Springer quickly put aside his self-consciousness about what they'd missed.

Within about three weeks, and without any involvement from me, there was breakfast ready at Mass every Sunday for anyone who wanted it. And I remember, one Sunday we started Mass with the clergy all robed and we processed down the center aisle of the sanctuary. And right there, in the center aisle of the sanctuary, were people still finishing breakfast!

So you had this opening hymn with the organ, and this procession, this kind of grand ceremony—not too grand in our church, but still. But the priests are in robes, and in the aisle in front of them were not just unhoused people but people finishing their breakfast and having conversation.

And that is an example of how one person's vision of something that matters to the whole community can come to life and not just come to life but affect our liturgical worship as well. It says, this is not about us having a cozy worship and then giving money to a homelessness ministry that we never see because it's on a Thursday. Now it's right there in the center aisle. They're having breakfast right now whilst you are trying to sing your hymn. It's wonderful, and it disturbs us. I think that's what the church in the neighborhood looks like at its best.[22]

For some worshipers, it is disturbing to have worship services interrupted that way. It is disturbing to center stories that typically sit at the margins and to treat them with the reverence often reserved for Scripture. It is disturbing for a straight-laced organization to tighten instead of loosen its connection with a neighborhood messy with real human struggle. But being disturbed is now part of the work of St. George-in-the-East. It's part of the everyday, communal process of witnessing the challenges that live right in front of them. It defines the opportunities that lie ahead.

Leading through the wilderness of this organizing experience has been disturbing for Springer, too, but in the best of ways.

Getting there involves putting people, stories, learning your own story and what matters to you, and putting other people's stories at the heart of what you do. For that woman who challenged us, her story was ten years of homelessness. She has a level of insight and understanding that I could never get to, no matter how much I care about the issue. So, let's listen to her and let's enable her to take up space in our church. Let's let her stand in her own power. And it made a difference—both for her and for our congregation.[23]

When prompted about his vision for the future of the congregation, Springer's response harks back to the reason he took this job in the first place: making the church part of God's work in the community. And he knows it won't happen overnight. At the baptism of a child whose parents joined the church after a long search for a spiritual home, the child's mother said out loud what she saw at St. George-in-the-East. "We looked at a lot of local churches. This one not only cared about affordable housing but was actually doing something about it. So we are here. That's why we came."

Springer reflects on that moment: "So people start to see. It starts to become not just individuals gaining power but the whole church-in-the-neighborhood gaining power and recognition and a good reputation. That's a reflection back on God. Obviously, in the end, that's what we're trying to do. The church is for everyone. Faith is for everybody that wishes to participate. And if you're not ready, we can go at your pace until you get there."

▲

Empowering Even "No":
Moses's Story

They have walked together hundreds of miles. The places where they enshrined miracles and milestones, the muddy bottom of the sea, days of hunger and thirst and fear, the slave quarters where the dream of this journey began—those are all behind them. Through all of it Moses led his people. He mediated for them when they angered their God. He forgave them when they complained endlessly. At the foot of Mount Sinai, where their thoughtless, stupid rebellion drew Moses into an anger so fierce he turned God's handwritten commandments into dust, even then Moses offered to sacrifice himself for their sake. "If you will not allow my people to enter the Promised Land," he contended with God, "then I will not go either. I am theirs and they are mine. Our end, our destination, is the same" (Exod 32:32, paraphrased).

And now they have reached this valley where they can actually see the river that moats the promised land. Their journey—thousands of days of purposeful steps forward and all those other days that felt like aimless wandering—is almost over. The land that holds for them the promise of freedom is finally, mercifully, in sight.

Over the forty years of this journey, two of the twelve Israelite tribes have managed to amass and care for herds of livestock—markers of wealth and power. They are Israelites, but their identity is hyphenated. They are Gadites and Reubenites, descendants of other sons of Isaac, sons who were not Joseph. They are independent thinkers; they have been nursing a quiet restlessness as Moses has called out directions from above. They have followed, but they have also been gathering for themselves capital not subject to Moses's direction.

A handful of leaders from these two tribes come to Moses one day as he sits in the command tent, planning the strategy for crossing the Jordan River to execute the final, triumphant part of their journey, the whole company's entry into the land of God's promise. They are almost home. "We think this—the territory on the nearer side of the Jordan—is the land that is best for our animals," the tribal leaders open. "The future of our tribes is best served by staying on this side of the river. You can go ahead and cross into Canaan, but we're going to stop here.

We'll build our homes, pen our sheep, and raise our children and grandchildren here. OK?" (Num 32:1–5, paraphrased).

This is not the first rebellion Moses has been confronted with. Once, with the promised land nowhere in sight, Korah, from the tribe of Levi, challenged the authority of both Moses and Aaron. Then, Moses knew exactly what to do. Deeper in the desert, order and obedience had to be maintained; the safety of the entire company was at risk. Moses's response was swift, and it was ruthless. Fourteen thousand seven hundred people were killed to reestablish Moses's prescribed authority; to him the cost seemed regrettable, but necessary (Num 16:1–32).

Now, Moses is startled; he did not see this coming. As the Gadite and Reubenite leaders sit waiting for his response, he is angry at first, just as he was when Korah challenged him. These ruffians are ungrateful, ignorant of what it has cost Moses to keep them safe all these years. They know nothing of what it will take to live outside the protection of God that Moses has secured for them. They are selfish, putting at risk not only their own tribes' future but the entire exodus project that the Israelites have been in together. How dare they make this move now, when the people's collective resolve is most critical?

Moses's first reactions reveal the hot-headedness that has always been his trademark. Unfiltered anger is the prerogative of a leader whose place at the top is secure. "Why will you turn the minds of the Israelites from crossing into the land that God has given them?" (Num 32:7). Why do you think your interests bear any consideration, when they weaken the project I am leading? Moses takes just a breath before he goes on, long enough to marshal and repackage the arguments of history. "Your ancestors did something like this once before. God punished them; it's their fault that this journey has been as long and hard as it has been. You are doing the same thing again" (Num 32:8–14, paraphrased). He threatens, "If you turn away from [God], who then abandons them once more in the wilderness, you will bring calamity upon all this people" (Num 32:15). Moses has brought down all the hammers within reach, including the threat of God's indiscriminate wrath, in his frenzy to smash back into place these willful, unruly subordinates.

In the sleepless nights that follow, Moses unravels the emotional knot inside himself. He is disappointed: What does it say about him if his leadership delivers to Canaan only ten tribes instead of the twelve that make a whole Israelite people? He is afraid: What if others follow those who have chosen to stay behind? Perhaps he is chastened: these tribes are not simply instruments of the promise that Moses has heard. Perhaps God has made another promise to them.

There are a few days of tense standoff. Moses and the tribal leaders avoid eye contact; they stay out of each other's way. Moses wonders whether the camp is swimming with seditious conversations that he cannot hear. He cannot help but suspect that a referendum on his leadership is brewing, unfairly, ungratefully. It is, surprisingly, the Reubenite and Gadite leaders who break the silence to find Moses again. They are the ones who come with a proposal for compromise. "Our families will stay here," they insist. "But then our men will come and fight with you for the land that you have been promised. We will cross the river with you into Canaan; we will do everything we can to see the rest of the Israelites installed in the promised land. And then we will return home to this land that will be ours" (Num 32:16–19, paraphrased).

The text suggests that Moses sputters a little; he repeats their proposal in words that recast as his command what they have already offered. The tribal leaders relent; they will fight for the land alongside their Israelite brothers. They will cross the Jordan to assert the promise to Moses that they will not claim for themselves. And then they will retreat. They will go back across the river to another land, a different promise (Num 32:20–32; see also Deut 3:18–20).

Even here, within arm's length of the end of the Israelites' journey, at the near edge of the promise God entrusted to him (not them!), Moses's singular hold on leadership is challenged. Even now, Moses is learning something he did not know before about his people's freedom. "The ultimate act of leadership is to bind oneself to a people who cannot be expected to reciprocate."[24] This is a people who hear and will continue to hear a promise that belongs to them. Sometimes it is the promise Moses has heard for them; sometimes it is not. Moses is not always the one who will judge which promise is truer. His leadership will be messy, all the way to the end. A once-certain vision of the future, now broken into pieces.

Notes

1   Michael Mather, *Having Nothing, Possessing Everything: Finding Abundant Communities in Unexpected Places* (Grand Rapids: Eerdmans, 2018), 20.

2   De'Amon Harges, interview, September 22, 2022.

3   Harges, interview.

4   Mather, *Having Nothing, Possessing Everything*, 21.

5   "The Bottom-Up Revolution Is . . . a Roving Listener," Strong Towns, April 22, 2021, https://tinyurl.com/4r3ka668.

6   TedX Talks, "Making the Invisible Visible," YouTube, 2015, https://tinyurl.com/387xafez.

7   Mather, *Having Nothing, Possessing Everything*, 24.

8   DeAmon Harges, John Knight, and Peter Block, "The Neighborhood Is the Center," Abundant Community, August 4, 2020, https://tinyurl.com/4madsx7u.

9   Harges, in "Neighborhood Is the Center."

10 Harges, in "Neighborhood Is the Center."

11 Harges, in "Neighborhood Is the Center."

12 Richard Springer, interview, July 27, 2022.

13 Springer, interview.

14 British "housing estates" are commonly referred to as "projects" in the US.

15 Springer, interview.

16 Springer, interview.

17 "Zero sum" implies that one person can't gain power without another giving up a commensurate amount.

18 Springer, interview.

19 Springer, interview.

20 Springer, interview.

21 Springer, interview.

22 Springer, interview.

23 Springer, interview.

24 Aaron Wildavsky, *Moses as Political Leader* (Tel Aviv: Shalem Press, 2005), 202.

Interlogue: Picking Up the Pieces

Life must be lived forward, but it can only be understood backward.

—Søren Kierkegaard, *Journals* 4

Moses, see, he will not enter this land. He is sitting on the sidelines all shape-shifty and jazzed. He carries the desert in his limbs. On his face the remnants of a glow. The glow has seeped into his skeleton and will shine on.

—Natalie Lyalin, *The Moses Cycle*

There will be no triumphant, ceremonial arrival into the promised land for the Israelites. No lockstep processional as they cross the border that for so long has evaded them. No, it's too late for that. Even before the final battle at the near edge of Canaan, the fabric of their mission is frayed. The tribes of Reuben and Gad have chosen to remain east of this new Eden; so have other tribes, or what's left of them. Narrating the final chapters of their wilderness journey, Moses recites the defections; he names new pairings of land and Israelite occupants, all on the near—and in Moses's mind the wrong—side of the Jordan River, just short of the place where honey and milk have been promised to flow abundant (Deut 3:12–16).

Moses opens Deuteronomy's memoir with self-defense. This is the voice of a leader weary of the relentless work of holding together a people who have themselves tired of an endless journey, a vision long deferred. Some of them have begun to dream of an alternate future: a different, more particular promise. Moses must wonder: Is there an expiration date on God's promises? Is there a time when "a long obedience in the same direction" might give way so that a new obedience may emerge?[1]

He has heard definitively, from the mouth of God, that he will not enter the promised land with his people. He is unnerved by God's rebuke to his efforts, his personal investment in this forty-year journey. How could the heat of God's anger be directed at him, of all people? He is the victim here, caught between a demanding God and a recalcitrant people. And—for the record—this was a job he didn't want in the first place. Moses turns his blame toward the Israelites, whose faithlessness he has covered for again and again. "You doubted," he tells them, and because of that doubt,

> None other than your God, who goes before you, will fight for you, just as [God] did for you in Egypt before your very eyes, and in the wilderness, where you saw how your God carried you . . . until you came to this place. Yet for all that, you have no faith in your God . . . who . . . heard your loud complaint and, becoming angry, vowed:
> Not one of those involved, this evil generation, shall see the good land that I swore to give to your fathers. . . . Because of you God was incensed with me too, saying: You shall not enter it either. (Deut 1:30–37)

The affront to Moses's ego guides his response; he reaches first for reproach, only later toward self-reflection. Forty years of walking at the front of the congregation has helped him trust his calling, but he is still human.[2] He is the leader. This people would still be slaves were it not for him. For all the progress he has made, his ego still bears the pyramid's imprint, faint as it may be.

The biblical narrative suggests that it was not the people's faithlessness for which God held Moses accountable; it was his own. The story is told in Numbers 20, when the people were at Meribeh, only a small distance from the Jordan River. They were thirsty (again). They groused (again) that Moses had brought them out of slavery in Egypt only to kill them with hunger and thirst. The sound of it must have been like nails on a chalkboard for their frustrated leader. Moses and Aaron brought the complaints back to the tent where God met them. They prostrated themselves, embarrassed by their people's whining and mistrust, even now. God heard and spoke a new instruction for releasing water from the desert rock. "You and your brother Aaron take the rod and assemble the community, and before their very eyes order the rock to yield its water. Thus you shall produce water for them from the rock and provide drink for the congregation and their beasts" (Num 20:9).

Moses took the rod, and he and Aaron went outside, assembling the grumblers in front of the rock. "Listen, you rebels," he shouted. "Shall we get water for you out of this rock?" Moses raised the rod over his head and brought it down on the rock—not once, but twice.

The water flowed. The people drank. But not the way God had intended, specifically instructed. Moses had struck the rock in anger rather than spoken to it. We can taste his bitterness in the epithet "you rebels." At the end of the journey, God had intended grace, not rebuke. The people should have been allowed to see: even a word from God is enough to sustain and to transform. Now God is displeased. The consequences are severe. "God said to Moses and Aaron, 'Because you did not trust Me enough to affirm My sanctity in the sight of the Israelite people, therefore you shall not lead this congregation into the land that I have given them'" (Num 20:12).

To be fair, God's instructions may have been ambiguous; God had told Moses to take up his staff but not to use it. Moses had once before been commanded to strike at another rock to draw water from it (Exod 17:1–7). Perhaps God was simply done with the repressed anger, the curtness, that often accented Moses's interactions with the Israelites. With God, Moses had grown into the fluency of friendship. There was between them an ease of communication, an occasional eloquence. But he had never gotten over the clipped tone he used with the people God had entrusted to his care.

God's withholding of the promised reward was indeed harsh punishment. It was perhaps disproportionate to the misdeed, its consequence a human tragedy in and of itself. Franz Kafka writes of this forfeiture in his *Diaries*: "[It] can only be intended to illustrate how incomplete a moment is human life, incomplete because a life like this could last forever and still be nothing but a moment. Moses fails to enter Canaan not because his life is too short but because it is a human life."[3]

Moses is humiliated; his self-image as a leader in charge is in pieces. There is an echo in this disgrace. This is not unlike the moment at Sinai, after Moses smashed to the ground the tablets bearing what was to be a timeless covenant between God and the people named God's own. That time, Moses calmed his rage and climbed the mountain again, to face God with an ashamed awareness not only of his people's sin but of his own too. Back then he found God ready to forget. This time he does not. God has turned away from Moses.

And so, Moses turns vulnerably, authentically, toward his people, perhaps for the very first time. He speaks to them with an emotional candor he has not been able to summon before.

I pleaded with God at that time, saying, "O, Lord God, You who let Your servant see the first works of Your greatness and Your mighty hand, You whose powerful deeds no god in heaven or on earth can equal! Let me, I pray, cross over and see the good land on the other side of the Jordan, that good hill country, and the Lebanon." But God was wrathful with me on your account and would not listen to me. God said to me, "Enough! Never speak to Me of this matter again!" (Deut 3:23–26)

In her deeply insightful book *Moses: A Human Life*, Avivah Gottlieb Zornberg writes, "In the aftermath of a kind of rupture with God—who, for the first time, refuses to listen to him—Moses turns toward a new conversation with his people. God has closed one door and, implicitly, provokes him to open another door. Instead of a passion to cross over the Jordan, Moses is now possessed by a new passion—to reach across to his people before he dies."[4]

Moses's dejection represents the final shattering of the pyramid that he transported inside himself all the way from Egypt to the threshold of the promised land. Only now does he look up from the mirror to see his leadership reflected back at him. Only now does he see the gathered faces of a people who are, even in their occasional unruliness and incessant complaining, as committed to this endeavor, as hopeful about its promise, as he is.

Something shifts for Moses—silently, subtly. Now, in the final chapters of Deuteronomy, in the last months of his life, in the midst of what he knows to be his final sermon, we hear in Moses's words to his people a new tone. Until now he has commanded them, exhorted them, reproached them, as if he alone bore the weight of responsibility for their future. Now he speaks with a different lexicon. Moses's final speeches are full of words he used only sparingly before, words that define the people's relationship with their God in terms of love rather than command.[5] For the first time, he addresses them as persons responsible for their own moral well-being and decisions.

There is another difference noticeable in Moses's final messages to his people. He refers to himself as if he is a character in their history, rather than an omniscient, impersonal channel of God's presence. He retells their stories in his own voice, without need to report or claim God's decree. It is as if God's surprising reprimand has lifted from him the burden of divine authority; now he is only human, one of the Israelites rather than one set apart. He no longer has to defend his position as the singular, privileged messenger of divine will. This change in Moses evokes something new in the people he now faces. They are the same people whose complaining has irked him forever, but now he sees in them a different capacity—to listen and see for themselves, to know for themselves what he had thought he had to know for them. Perhaps they have changed—or perhaps the change is in Moses's eyes.

At the last, as the Israelites prepare to cross the Jordan River with Joshua in their lead rather than Moses, God predicts that once they enter the promised land, the Israelites will again lose their way. They will abandon the God who brought them safely through the wilderness; there will be other, shinier objects to love (Deut 31:16–21). Moses, for once, does not argue. He does not put on the familiar mantle of responsibility, either for the people or for God. They will all have to work it out for themselves. Instead he addresses the people directly:

> *Surely, this instruction which I enjoin upon you this day is not too baffling for you, nor is it beyond reach. It is not in the heavens, that you should say, "Who among us can go up to the heavens and get it for us and impart it to us, that we may observe it?" Neither is it beyond the sea, that you should say, "Who among us can cross to the other side of the sea and get it for us and impart it to us, that we may observe it?" No, the thing is very close to you, in your mouth and in your heart, to observe it.*
>
> *I call heaven and earth to witness against you this day: I have put before you life and death, blessing and curse. Choose life—if you and your offspring would live—by loving your God, heeding God's commands, and holding fast to [God]. For thereby you shall have life and shall long endure upon the soil that God swore to your fathers Abraham, Isaac, and Jacob, to give to them. (Deut 30:11–14, 19–20)*

As Moses acknowledges the people's agency—for the first time, they will master their own destiny—he, too, is transformed.

Now he is the leader whose work is to make room for every person's implication in God's calling and promise. Now he is the prophet whose life reflects the character of the liberating God. In the words of Zornberg: "His humanity is revealed to him in the wilderness: a personal life that finds expression in the speeches of his final months. The man of God who had always spoken for Israel now speaks for his personal self in a way that stirs depths in those who hear him. When he reaches out to his people in the fraught language of relationship, he makes himself unforgettable."[6]

Now, finally, Moses picks up the pieces of all that has broken along the way. His unassailable ego. His pharaonic image of a leader's singular command. His illusion that all the words from God's mouth would be spoken in Moses's voice. Here, at the threshold of the promised land, all those shards of brokenness— some polished, some jagged—lie on the ground. They are the remnants of an old way that had seemed unbreakable. Now the pieces are ready to be picked up, not by Moses alone but by all the people God has brought this far, to be carried side by side with the still-intact tablets now housed in the holy of holies. Broken and whole together. And some day, in time, those shards will be rearranged into a new mosaic, a picture of failures made full, of brokenness now blessed.

Notes

1 Eugene H. Peterson, *A Long Obedience in the Same Direction: Discipleship in an Instant Society* (Downers Grove, IL: InterVarsity, 2000).

2 Moses spoke of this to the people "in the fortieth year, on the first day of the eleventh month" (Deut 1:3).

3 Franz Kafka, *Diaries 1914–23*, trans. Martin Greenberg and Hannah Arendt (New York: Schocken Books, 1965), 195–96, quoted in Avivah Gottlieb Zornberg, *Moses: A Human Life* (New Haven: Yale University Press, 2016), 192.

4 Zornberg, *Moses: A Human Life*, 181–83.

5 Zornberg, *Moses: A Human Life*, 175.

6 Zornberg, *Moses: A Human Life*, 194.

Part III

Dreaming of the World Yet to Be

CHAPTER NINE

Mosaic Leadership

Confessions of a Recovering Dragon: Kathi's Story

Before I entered seminary, I practiced law. I was a civil litigator, one of those lawyers whose work is either inside or preparing to be inside a courtroom, where we argue our client's worth and an opponent's lack thereof—all trying to make someone pay for the immeasurable loss of a broken relationship. For most of the fifteen years I worked as a lawyer, I supervised a team of associates who worked under me on the firm's cases. For the most part, these were people I had hired myself. I'd chosen them from a pool of applicants because they seemed to me the best educated, most experienced, and most likely to work with the kind of intensity and excellence that I wanted our clients to be able to count on. Excellence was important to me, and I wanted my associates to do our clients proud. To do me proud.

No matter what it looks like on television, the truth is that most litigation is resolved on the basis of written arguments. So written work—legal briefs, memos, even letters—is the most visible and critical part of a litigator's daily work. This is where I expected my team to shine. Our writing had to be smart, concise, thoroughly researched, even stylish, for me to be satisfied with it. I insisted on it. No piece of paper (we still used paper then) would leave our office before it met my exacting standard. That meant I did a lot of late-night rewriting. I also did a lot of critiquing. I often (always?) found some shortcoming in my associates' work. The reasoning was weak, or the writing was sloppy, or a strategic point had been missed. Almost no one could consistently meet my expectations.

And so, one by one, those associates would leave, sometimes just before I planned to fire them. After all, no one works well under the gaze of constant disappointment. Our firm became known for the quality of its work product, but the cost of that reputation was high. In my impatience with the slow, natural progress of training and professional growth, I temporarily derailed the legal careers of a good handful of people who were just trying to do the best they could. I look back at that part of my professional career with no small modicum of shame. I understand and still appreciate the value of excellent work and consistent productivity. Sometimes it can feel necessary. But I wish I had stopped to consider the worth of those persons more thoughtfully and as more than just extensions of my professional ambition.

I was not a person of faith in those years. I'd like to think that I would never treat people like that again, now that I am more conscious of the Christian gospel's imperative on my life. It is a tension, holding our big hopes for the organizations we lead together with a generous, unwavering regard for the dignity and God-given worthiness of every person. I still have to catch myself, consciously, when my impatience threatens to surface. But there is another voice in my head now, one that says, "No piece of work matters more than the people who are doing it."

"We Have to Completely Rethink the Industry"

On January 9, 2023, a front-page headline in the *New York Times* announced, "Noma, Rated the World's Best Restaurant, Is Closing Its Doors."[1] In the rarified world of elite restaurants, this was a seismic event. Noma, the luxury food mecca in Copenhagen, had been named the world's best restaurant so many times that it had exhausted its eligibility to win the title again. Hundreds of people every year planned their travels around a pilgrimage to a dinner table there. Surely Noma could have moved on to a long life of sustained profitability and perhaps even more ethereal awards and accolades. Instead, Noma's head chef and creative genius, Rene Redzepi, announced that the restaurant would close its doors as soon as it finished its current commitments.

The reason for Noma's closing, Redzepi said, was that he'd had enough. It's not hard to imagine that providing customers with luxurious, conversation-worthy meals every night must be exhausting. The high culture of creative dining requires back-breaking work; it's relentless in its demand for soul-draining and body-killing discipline—not only from the chef but from every person in and around that kitchen. We've seen it on reality TV: exacting chefs stressed beyond human limits channeling their anxiety into attacks on the spirits of line workers. Under that kind of pressure, everyone's humanity corrodes.

Redzepi told the *Times* it was the breathing space imposed on him by Covid that cleared his head enough to question the industry's business model. But he'd already begun to question the culture in which he'd grown up as a chef. The only way he knew how to lead a kitchen was the way he'd been trained himself. Amid buzzing activity, a professional kitchen is a diagram of perfect order. Everyone knows their place; every function is tightly monitored. No one defies the chef's orders, either publicly or privately. Redzepi had learned by watching other chefs, who rule their kitchens with clenched fists and loud voices, bullying and humiliating lower-order cooks into making and repeating perfection. The spectacle of gourmet chefs harassing subordinates—barking out aggressive instructions, demanding exquisitely detailed obedience—is so predictable that it's become a whole genre of entertainment unto itself.

The method has persisted because it works. Restaurants reached their gilded age in the 1990s and early decades of the twenty-first century.[2] But the cost has been high. Years of shouting in the kitchen carved out a path for the misogyny and machismo that destroy collegial culture, elevated (almost exclusively) men to the upper echelons, and rewarded abusive behavior. Young people who thought they wanted to spend their lives cooking burned out before turning thirty, or they simply walked away before the burnout set in. Experts and industry elders like Redzepi are leaving the work they once felt called to. In a thought-provoking essay addressed to his colleagues in 2015, Redzepi urged, "The only way we will be able to reap the promise of the present is by confronting the unpleasant legacies of our past, and collectively forging a new path forward."[3]

Eight years later, apparently, Redzepi had lost hope that he or his fellow chefs could muster the will to change the culture of professional kitchens. "We have to completely rethink the industry," he told a *New York Times* reporter who interviewed him about his decision to close.[4] He hadn't been able to figure out how to lead a world-class restaurant kitchen differently. And most discouraging to Redzepi, it looked like neither had anyone else.

Restaurants are not churches, and religious leaders are not chefs. But pyramid-like structures still tower over both systems: one branded by the offer of an unparalleled experience of fine dining, the other an institution that promises divinely inspired wisdom. The image of a creative genius with unquestionable professional expertise has stamped itself on our expectations of chefs and religious leaders both. It explains at least some of the inhumanity we're willing to forgive them for. But is this kind of workplace failure a fait accompli, as Redzepi has concluded? Or might there be another path forward?

Another Way: Mosaic Leadership

In virtually every industry, there are at least a few leaders who know that organizational effectiveness does not require tamping down the creative instincts of the people around them and corralling employees and volunteers inside a box on the org chart. These are unconventional leaders who trust that effective leadership does not have to wear you down to the bone. Margaret Wheatley calls this model of leadership the new story. "Leaders who live in the new story help us understand ourselves differently by the way they lead. They trust our humanness; they welcome the surprises we bring to them; they are curious about our differences; they delight in our inventiveness; they nurture us; they connect us."[5]

These are Mosaic leaders. They are leaders who have learned—sometimes through hard-won lessons like Moses's—that coercive control only breeds passivity, resistance, resentment, and abdication of responsibility. Mosaic leaders rely not solely on their own instincts but on the collective vision of the room. They piece together disparate refractions of that vision until the angle of its reflection is wide.

Mosaic leaders attend to the moments when another voice, an alternative point of view or a fresh set of gifts, is called for. They make room for others to rise up and speak into those moments. They are generous in sharing the power that comes with their position, constantly seeking out partners in a common cause, trusting others to hold responsibility with them, holding lightly to their authority, their standing, and their influence. They measure the success of their leadership not exclusively by the accomplishment of a metrics-driven set of organizational goals but by the fullness of satisfaction and employment of gifts the work brings to the people engaged—as workers, as partners, even as those served.

Mosaic Leadership: What It Is *Not*

Mosaic leadership is not a method, a mindset, or a program. It's a dialect of the language of leadership more widely spoken and understood. It's authority exercised with an eye toward sharing power rather than hoarding it, knowing that power used for good is an abundant, renewable resource. It is a leadership stance with a distinctive tilt to it; it leans toward empowering other people.

Mosaic leadership is sometimes best identified not by what it is but by what it decidedly is not. Wheatley has been a careful observer of organizational culture for a long time. In her 2005 book *Finding Our Way*, she describes cultural patterns that are distinctly non-Mosaic:

> For too long we've been treating people as machines. We've tried to force people into tiny boxes, called roles and job descriptions. We've told people what to do and how they should behave. We've believed we could "re-engineer" organizations to be efficient machines and treated people as replaceable parts in the machinery of production.
>
> Trying to be an effective leader in this machine story is especially exhausting. He or she is leading a group of lifeless, empty automatons who are just waiting to be filled with vision and direction and intelligence. The leader is responsible for providing everything: the organizational mission and values, the organizational structure, the plans, the supervision. The leader must also figure out through clever use of incentives or coercives, how to pump energy into the lifeless mass. Once the pump is primed, he must then rush hither and yon to make sure that everyone is clanking along in the same direction at the established speed, with no diversions. It is the role of the leader to provide organizing energy for a system that is believed to have no internal capacities for self-creation, self-organization, or self-correction.[6]

This is the old story, the empire's story. We can see its effects, Wheatley says, in a not-unfamiliar image: "people in the organization ready and willing to do good work, wanting to contribute their ideas, ready to take responsibility, and leaders holding them back, insisting that they wait for decisions or instructions. The result is dispirited employees [or volunteers] and leaders wondering why no one takes responsibility or gets engaged anymore."[7]

There is a new story, but like every countercultural narrative, becoming a part of that story demands the courage to let go of old habits, often before you've adopted new ones to replace them.

Becoming a Mosaic Leader

Like Moses, the leadership lessons of pyramid culture are deeply embedded in us. There is unlearning to do first, to dislodge the pharaonic impulses now embedded in us, to let go of the lofty ambitions inspired by an inhuman (and inhumane) productivity culture. And unlike the Israelites' midnight departure into exodus, this transformation of character most certainly does not take place overnight. Formation as a Mosaic leader is a matter of *becoming*: it is piecemeal growth, cultivated in hard and humbling experiences of letting go and picking up alike.

Like tiled artwork, Mosaic leadership is pieced together. It's rearranged from the broken remnants of a vessel that once seemed unbreakable, made out of our good intentions, our well-honed intuitions, our vision for the work we invested ourselves in. Even these most trustworthy traits are fragile, it turns out. They can shatter under the weight of leadership's relentless demands—on you and on your people

We are returned, again and again, to the wilderness. There our inherited self-image is tested, tried, and trimmed. There our clenched fists slowly unfurl, soften in response to graces that come not of our own doing. And, as it turns out, there are no shortcuts.

Practices of Mosaic Leaders

Mosaic leaders are formed by practices. These are not leadership hacks; they are more like spiritual disciplines, designed to spiral constantly toward self-reflection, humility, and compassion. The work is patient and it is personal. It will change you before it changes anything else. But as you feel something internal shift—dislodge, perhaps—by these practices, so will the people you lead.

Cultivate Curiosity

Curiosity, an open and inquisitive wondering about what might be, is a foundational quality of a Mosaic leader-in-transformation. It steers toward honest introspection (why did I respond that way?), collaboration (how might this look through someone else's eyes?), and a modest deference to all that is not yet known (what gifts am I not yet seeing?). Curiosity is the key to every passageway out, just as its opposite—certainty—ensures that you'll remain locked inside the way things are. But it requires you to hold your own ideas, and sometimes yourself, ever so lightly. Doing that will open possibilities you had not calculated and summon surprises you might otherwise have strategized out of possibility. Curiosity opens the way to wonder: at the magnificence of a world that does not require your operation and at the truth that you are not alone in your passion to drive change.

Think of Moses on the first morning when manna appeared. He had prayed for sustenance for his people; he had great confidence that God would come through somehow. Surely he too pictured fleshpots—just like those from his upbringing in Egypt—in his praying mind's eye. He had no idea what would happen next. And when manna fell to the earth, a miraculous but entirely mysterious substance, he too thought "What is it?" (in Hebrew, *mah na*) was the perfect name for the odd, flaky, disappearing bread that fell from the sky. What more fitting name could there be to name his curiosity: a question rather than an answer?

Center the Marginal

Welcoming strangers to the center of your community is more than a matter of doing the right thing. Expanding your thinking to include foreign thoughts is not just a maxim of disruptive innovation. Embracing difference makes your work better. So how do you do it? Solicit the opinions and ideas that line the margins of your organization, from the people who usually speak their thoughts only in the parking lot, or in whispered tones, or not at all. These are the voices that carry the sounds you need to hear even before your supporters'. The outsiders who are most apt to agitate because "they just don't understand how we do things" have the insights that can crack you open to see something you haven't been able to see before. Invite them in. Give them a meaningful voice—not just about the details of what you've already planned but about what's at the heart of the matter.

This is Moses as he watches Nachshon step from the back of the crowd at the edge of the sea and walk into the roiling Red Sea. Nachshon wades in with no experience at leading, no learned deference to the power of chaotic waves. The water rises to his shoulders and then his nose; his is a foolish bravery. But soon enough, to Moses's surprise, too, the tide turns.

Trust Your People

Trust them so much that it makes you uncomfortable. And then trust them more. Trust their opinions. Trust their ability to produce important deliverables. Trust them to care about the mission of the organization as much as you do. Bet heavily on the truth of this proposition: people will rise to the height of your demonstrated expectations of them. If they have become accustomed to silently managing up, expecting the leader to shoulder responsibility for all the decisions and the work to implement those decisions, it may be a long, slow road back to partnership. But you can start it by engaging them in substantive discussions and trusting them to offer a meaningful contribution.

When Yitro advised Moses to turn over to others his weekly calendar of adjudicating disputes among the people, no doubt

Moses worried. No one else could do that work with the care and wisdom he'd accumulated himself. But self-governance was a critical skill for the Israelites, and shared authority was a necessary step in Moses's evolution toward Mosaic leadership.

Ask More (and Better) Questions

Often we think that the leader is the one who should have all the answers. But Mosaic leaders know that not every question needs to be answered, and the questions that matter most can't be answered with solutions or easy answers. Your job is to help people make meaning from their experiences, to inspire a thoughtful, faithful, creative response to the challenges before them. You do this by asking good questions and listening carefully to how people answer—which usually leads to more questions. Open a sustained conversation about your organization's purpose in a changing world. Ask questions you don't know the answers to, like: Why are we doing this work? Is it important? Why is it important?'

When Moses turned to the Israelites before they entered the promised land at the edge of the Jordan River, he did not offer them rules of thumb or a detailed map forward. He invited them to ask: Who are we? What matters to us? And then he reminded them: "The word is very close to you. It's in your mouth and in your heart, waiting for you to do it" (Deut 30:14). He was inviting them to ponder, to stay in the questions until answers emerged from inside them.

Embrace the Ad Hoc

Often, the organizations and institutions we inherit are weighed down by rules and processes that restrict movement. Not every decision that was right in its moment merits being codified into a bylaw. Nonessential rules and traditions are barriers to change. They restrict new thoughts. They inadvertently obstruct new people from entering. From the outside, the system can look like a lockbox, with only a handful of keys distributed to the chosen few. Mosaic leaders decode the things that do not deserve to be shrouded in such mystery. In your work, practice making rules only when absolutely necessary, and keep them simple. Resist the urge to cement your response into policy, to establish a tradition before it is ripe, to pronounce an "always" when a "for now" will suffice.

Moses's final instruction, "Choose life," said everything that needed to be said. Allowing your people and your organization to flex and bend and flow will free them—and you—to choose life as it presents itself, not as it was one time before.

Slow Down
The famous late-stage-capitalist Silicon Valley motto to move fast and break things is good for disrupting the status quo, but it leaves a lot of broken bodies in its wake. Mosaic leaders are mindful that the well-being of a whole ecosystem is at stake with every decision. Practice deliberately slowing the pace of your thinking, your actions, and the exercise of your opinions. Leave space for self-reflection, and allow for delayed revelations to refine your raw intuition. Slowing down will give your spirit a chance to catch up with your strategy. Use the pause to appreciate the contributions of others before you hurry to position your bricks atop theirs, before the mortar has had a chance to dry.

Forty years Moses and his band of Israelites wandered through the desert, the story goes, on a trip that might have taken two weeks as the crow flies. Their excruciatingly long stay in the wilderness formed them into a people who understood themselves and one another. Repetitions of complaint and conflict and reconciliation chiseled Moses into the leader God had always imagined he could be. It takes time to develop clarity and courage.

Use Your Power to Bless Others

To bless something is to pronounce it good, just as it is, without wishing for its alteration. Prayer in the Mosaic tradition often begins with humans blessing God.

Baruch Ata Adonai, Yodeah Razim.

Blessed are you, God, who knows the secrets of people.

This is the Jewish prayer said when a large crowd gathers and acknowledges that only God can know what secrets lie in the hearts of each person. Only the Knower of Secrets can see the yearnings inside each person, the gifts they've got, the hopes they hold, the possibilities they possess. There is an odd sort of power dynamic at work here: How is it that a people below bless the God above? It takes power to bless another. But that power can be offered from any position, and it can be exercised to honor—to stand under, even in awe of—the one who is being blessed.

The power required to bless someone is not institutional. It does not even have to be religious. You do not have to be ordained, or holy in some way yourself, before you can be a blesser. When humans bless one another, it is a declaration that says to the blessee: "I see you. And what I see in you is beyond judgment." Imagine how that message, even implicit, sounds in the ear, especially when it comes from a leader who bears respect.

In the words of the poet Pádraig Ó Tuama, a blessing says simply, "Let me wrap you in a word that is meant for pure goodness."[8] Anyone can do this. You can do this. So do it. Because when you bless someone, when you see and express confidence in their goodness, in something in them they may not yet see for themselves, they stand a little taller. They turn their eyes to look in the same direction you are looking, trying to see what you see, and perhaps even something you don't see yet. They join you in the holy work you thought you had to do alone.

Notes

1 Julia Moskin, "Noma, Rated the World's Best Restaurant, Is Closing Its Doors," *New York Times*, January 9, 2023, https://tinyurl.com/ydcn7cxn.
2 Moskin, "Noma, Rated the World's Best Restaurant."
3 Rene Redzepi, "Culture of the Kitchen," MAD, August 19, 2015, https://tinyurl.com/bdd3c275.
4 Moskin, "Noma, Rated the World's Best Restaurant."
5 Margaret J. Wheatley, *Finding Our Way* (Oakland, CA: Berrett-Koehler, 2005), 30.
6 Wheatley, *Finding Our Way*, 20.
7 Wheatley, *Finding Our Way*, 64.
8 Pádraig Ó Tuama, *Poetry Unbound: 50 Poems to Open Your World* (New York: Norton, 2022), 201.

CHAPTER TEN

Are We There Yet?

The 120-Year-Old Desk: Elan's Story

Almost two decades ago, I stood at an early career crossroads, deciding between two paths that called to me: human-rights law and a career in the rabbinate. I wasn't all that certain that I was qualified to do either, but I thought I should at least figure out whether I could see myself growing into either vocation. And, in retrospect, I now see that it was no coincidence that my search began just about a year after losing my father. This wasn't just a search for a career; it was a search for purpose.

I spent several months taking a day off here, a half-day there. I visited all the rabbis and lawyers who were kind enough to answer my call then show me around their workplaces and answer my many questions. My search was exhausting, but by the end of it I felt deeply energized, renewed by the generosity of family friends, childhood rabbis, and strangers who were eager to pull back the curtain on their careers and share reflections with an up-and-coming potential colleague.

The funny thing is that I saw inklings of my purpose in both vocations. Not because of what I saw in the career paths of the lawyers and rabbis who showed me around, but rather because of how they did so—with tremendous grace and generosity of spirit, whether I was being welcomed into a rich, oak-paneled law office or a rabbi's study walled with towering shelves of ancient texts.

But there was one visit, with one rabbi in particular, that ultimately drew me toward the rabbinate. This rabbi, the last one I visited, rescheduled multiple times (with heartfelt apology) before our visit took place. First there was an unexpected, closed-door executive session of her synagogue's board. Then a funeral of a beloved congregant. Then an interfaith community vigil.

When our meeting time finally came, I pulled into the synagogue parking lot and gathered myself a bit before walking up the steps to the front door. Having grown up in a lay-led *minyan* community that met inside a small, humble church, this building felt profoundly imposing. Perhaps anticipating this, the rabbi met me right at the entrance, handed me a cup of hot coffee, and walked me around the building before we ended up in her stately office. There we spent several hours in conversation while she fended off a handful of door knocks and intercom pings. The topics of conversation ranged from her childhood to her first moment of calling, to the ups and downs of serving as the senior rabbi in a large, demanding pulpit, to the many lessons she had learned over decades in the rabbinate. She came across as the same honest, wise, and vulnerable person that she did when I had seen her preach in front of hundreds of her congregants. There was no daylight between her public persona—kind, wise, grounded—and the rabbi who treated me like a trusted colleague that day.

At one point, after she'd run through a list of several ambitious initiatives she and her colleagues were juggling at the time, I took the risk of asking her whether she was worried about the many renovations that the building clearly needed. During our brief tour, she'd offered a sort of apology about whatever in sight was showing signs of wear and tear: the sanctuary needed a fresh coat of paint, the social hall was showing its age, the classrooms needed smart boards and other technology. She opened her mouth to respond, but before a word came out, she paused and smiled to herself. Then she told me a story. "Once upon a time," she said,

> I sat in this same chair on my first day of work here, right in front of this same massive desk. Back when I was interviewing

for this job, my predecessor here showed me this desk, walnut, 120 years old, the first piece of furniture they brought into this building. It's so old that there's a buzzer under its top, with a line that runs underneath the floor into my assistant's office. The first rabbi used to buzz it to summon his secretary to come in and take dictation when he was writing his sermons.

And here I was on my first day of work, sitting at the same desk, staring at a fresh legal pad in front of me. The first thing I wrote down was a long list of things I could see my predecessor had let wither under his watch. The façade of the building was cracking. The youth group was leaderless. The board was rudderless. Membership numbers had been in decline for years. Those were the first things I got to work on.

When I finished writing the list, I wrote another note: a letter to myself, promising that I would never do what he did. I would never let any facet of this synagogue—the programs, the people, the plant—fall behind. Not on my watch.

And you know what? Here I sit, in the very same chair in front of the very same desk, all these years later. I'm proud to say we've made great strides on the things I wrote on my first list. But, if I'm being totally honest, we both know the building needs work. Some of our programs could use fine-tuning and some fresh energy. And if—God forbid—I surveyed our congregants and asked them what they thought of the job I've done, I'd hear more than an earful about what more I should be doing.

My prayer is that someday, not all that long from now, someone like you will sit at this very same desk and write on a fresh legal pad a long list of all the things I didn't tend to while I served here, and then tackle them with love and dedication—even if they're mumbling under their breath about what I should have done differently. Nothing would give me greater satisfaction than that.

So if you're asking me today if I would do it all over again, or if I think you should consider the rabbinate for yourself, my answer is a wholehearted and resounding "Yes!" This has been the most rewarding career I could have ever imagined. God has been so, so good to me, even in all the painful and challenging moments along the way. But, Elan, you need to know this: the work is never done.

Taking It as Far as We Can

Moses spent his last leadership years knowing when and where his journey would end. No other achievement would change the edict that his last steps would be taken at the doorstep to the promised land, not inside it. He would take his final breath so close to the border that he could taste in the air faint hints of the milk and honey once promised to him and his people. A whole book of midrash imagines his persistent negotiations with God to be granted just one more step,[1] just one more day, but in the end Moses accepts his fate gracefully. He climbs to the highest point he can find, gazes on the land from afar one last time, and passes on.

No one else's journey will look exactly like Moses's, but the end of his story is universal. None of us will make it into the promised land. Few of us will pronounce a mission singularly accomplished, at least not without paying the price of failing at a variety of others. Most of us will work as hard as we can, give as much as we're able to give, and pray that it's enough—pray that *we* are enough.

But what is enough in our day? One of the subtle harms done to us by an empire mindset is the consistent message that whatever we are, we are not enough. Whatever we've accomplished, we could have always done more. No matter how big the community, it should be just a little bit bigger before we can finally retire feeling satisfied and accomplished. One more Fund the Future campaign should make the endowment large enough. And no matter how divine the building, just one more renovation will make it truly worthy of serving as a dwelling place for God.

How do we measure the success of our work when the metrics available to us only tell a tiny portion of the story? Congregational numbers might indicate a slight uptick in membership or attendance. Meeting ambitious building and fundraising goals might make a small dent in an endless need. But these are not the metrics that will tell an authentic story of our lives or reveal the convictions that drew us to this work.

Our most meaning-laden efforts will always point toward achievements that are ephemeral. Like Moses's journey, however close we might get to the border of success, we will never quite cross over. At our best, we take strides toward the potential that lies before us and the organizations we lead; at our worst, our progress is measured in inches rather than yards. Our story always ends, like Moses's, just shy of the promised land's border. Mosaic leadership does not magnify that marker. It simply internalizes a message that is more powerfully transformative: even failures are progress, so long as we gather them up and carry them with us.

Virtuous Cycles

In Jewish communities, the five books of the Torah are read as a cycle that ends and begins right after Rosh Hashanah, the Jewish New Year. Year after year, the Torah begins again, and so do we. There is only the slightest pause between Moses's last words in Deuteronomy and God's first ones in Genesis. On Simchat Torah,[2] in the midst of joyous singing and dancing, Torah scrolls are unfurled, each parchment piece held delicately by community members encircling the sanctuary. There, in full view for everyone to witness, the story of creation leads right into the first family strife, which flows into the flood, the birth of Judaism, the Israelites' enslavement by a cruel new pharaoh, and so on, until Moses takes his last breath in the wilderness. And there, on the next parchment over, held shoulder to shoulder with the final one reciting Moses's death, the story of creation begins again.

This is the cycle of Mosaic leadership, too. The great leader Moses was made neither at his journey's origin, in Egypt, nor at its end, in the promised land. He and his people were transformed throughout a cycle that moved from the dream of liberation to the dream's renewal a generation later. In between, they encountered a great and disturbing wilderness. Likewise, our work as leaders is not linear; there is no beginning or end to it. We cycle through its chapters over and over again, spiraling onward—upward and downward both—through the wilderness. Every turn retreads familiar ground while it moves us closer to an envisioned promise ahead.

The Mosaic Leadership Cycle: Dreaming, Disturbing, Distancing

This is the cycle that carries us through each form of wilderness we encounter in our life's journey. It reminds us that even as the last dream fades, even when we venture out a long way from home, even when we find the promised land guarded by a closed door, we are not spinning out of the universe's control. We are, in fact, exactly where we most need to be.

Dreaming

The first stage of the Mosaic leadership cycle draws from its final scene: a dream. Every great journey begins with a dream. The kind of prophetic dream that awakens the dreamer to possibilities that stir and spark the actions that might manifest them.

Moses's final sermon to his people is a retelling of the dream of freedom that urged them forward from the beginning. Sure, it rehashes old stories, even relitigates old fights. But the resounding message of Moses's words is a charge to the Israelites to hold onto hope, to be informed by the experiences of their past, to let themselves be inspired again to build a world on the other side of the border worthy of their struggles on this one.

This is what Mosaic leaders do. In the wilderness of his own professional transition, Eugene Kim, the founder of New Wine

Collective, looks around at a landscape now visible in panoramic perspective. Here, outside the confines of the church built by his own hands, he is truly free to dream a bigger, clearer dream. Now, he says, "My ultimate hope for New Wine isn't a single community of faith; it's system change. Our hope is to create a whole new ecosystem for spiritual communities that can sustain all kinds of life and be a part of healing the world."[3]

Maurice Winley's early dream for Living Redemption has yielded to the prophetic project of building a more worthy world for young Black men in his community and even beyond it: "To dream of a better humanity, a divine humanity—that's what it means to be created in *imago Dei*.[4] To dream of equity. Why should there be anyone hungry? Why should there be anyone without a home and without whatever they need to live in dignity? This earth is abundant. Why can't we all share in its abundance and appreciate the uniqueness and the diversity that God has invested in all of creation?"[5]

It's not the content of a dream that is critical to Mosiac leadership; it's the conviction of the leader to keep dreaming. Lack of imagination is what kept the Israelites tethered to the place of their slavery in the early years of their exodus. And then, once they crossed the border into Canaan, an inherited memory of comfort and stability quickly took the place of the vision that had propelled them through the wilderness. Complacency was the temptation that lurked close behind them. It drew them back too quickly into the captivity of kingship—the very system they had once escaped.

But even the most vivid dreams fade over time. Perhaps this is a signal that it is time to retire the last vision to make room for the next. Holding a new vision alongside a long-cherished one keeps us from falling too deeply in love with the past or grasping too desperately toward the future. Sometimes there is a natural harmony. But sometimes different, even opposing, dreams must be held next to one another, even in their uneasy tension. This, too, is the I'll-go-first work of a leader.

"Yes... and" is a phrase that links the last dream to the next one. Improvisational comedy lends us this small tool, from its tradition of leaping from one creative thought to its unlikely progeny. Two small words reassure us that we can hold a new dream without the old one crashing carelessly to the ground. They invite holding onto the world as it is ("Yes") and imagining the world as it is yet to be ("and").

Disturbing

In every visioning process, there is a moment when the excitement of the dream gets outmatched by the urgent rhythms of routine. Try as we might to stay in the warm embrace of a delightful dream, morning always comes. We stir to witness the world-as-it-is coming back to life, reality settling in like dew on our dreamscape. Vision yields to vicissitudes, and before we know it, we are once again held captive by our compulsive efforts to sustain the present. The impulse doesn't feel all that constraining at first; it seems necessary. But the tyranny of "but what about...?" is more than a wake-up call. It can be a death knell to a daring idea.

In organizational life, this is the moment when we can become indentured again. Sometimes it takes a generation to see what has happened; or, if the current toward change runs strong, someone might speak a protest immediately. But we are prone to accommodate our captor. It's a voice that sounds eminently prudent. Before we know it, we are back to work making bricks—until the cycle begins again and we shift into the holy task of disturbing ourselves toward a new freedom.

The pattern is perennial; it repeats itself even in communities that have experienced their own transformation most consciously. Richard Springer says of his congregation at St. George-in-the-East, "We need to disorganize, disturb ourselves.

We were really quite energetic throughout the pandemic, and now we need to loop back around to the next stage in the cycle. In our church, we're definitely primed for a period of disturbing the present. It's an exciting stage to be in."[6]

Disturbing the status quo, of course, is not merely an outward act. Our call is to disturb ourselves, too, even if that means sacrificing comfort, predictability, or status. Empire culture is so intricately woven into our organizations and our everyday lives that it is impossible to hold a position of power and not benefit in some way from the system as it is. To disturb that system is a risk for every leader. But the promise of the wilderness ahead is too great to forestall breaking out from the present.

Positioning ourselves where we can scan the horizon for signs of disturbance, and then welcome it, requires a conscious choice to live with some dis-ease. Rabbi Sara Luria describes it:

> You have to want to not be part of the status quo more than you want to be part of the status quo in order to do any kind of disturbing. And, in fact, you have to recognize—like Moses did—that maybe you're not part of the normative, dominant culture. As comfortable as you might be knowing what each day will bring, living well in the world as it is, you have to look inward like Moses did, and decide, "I am never going to be Egyptian." My whole history, my whole lineage, my whole heart is not a "status quo" kind of heart.[7]

Disturbance temporarily unmoors the present from its past. It's important to remember that the discomfort of disturbance is a liminal state—just for now. It's the prod we need to get us moving toward the wilderness, where transformation can do its work in us. When we find ourselves and our communities in this uneasy state, "for now" is a useful phrase. It is a nonpartisan arbiter; it promises neither return to the former things nor a specific future. "For now" promises that this, too, will pass. We are reminded that both the moments of peace and calm and the times of tumult and struggle are temporary. It is equanimity we need, not a return to stillness. And for now—while disturbance is our most insistent companion—all the things we feel in its discomfort are true and meaningful, and they are reshaping us.

Distancing

Revelation, like liberation, doesn't come immediately upon stepping foot into the wilderness. It's rarely accompanied by thunder and lightning. We may not absorb it in real time, maybe not even the second time it is offered to us. But the more we distance ourselves from the confines of our familiarity, the more receptive we become, and the more likely we are to receive God's new thing when it makes itself evident again. God speaks to us in all manner of ways—in the echoing cry of a movement rally, through a congregant's story confided in passing, in a grain of truth buried inside the anger of a disappointed neighbor. Whether we are able to receive these messages depends entirely on how far into the wilderness we have yet ventured.

We have to go a long way into the wilderness before we are beyond nostalgia's long reach. This is where all Mosaic leaders are made, including Moses himself. This is where the unknown forces us to wrestle with the truths we have not yet taken in. It's where old dreams grow faint enough to leave space for new ones to emerge, where the echoes of traditions past make way for innovations not yet fully formed. Adam Kligfeld knows something of sojourning for a long while in the wilderness. Thirteen years after traveling across the country to take a strange, new role, he remembers what he took from that powerful experience of not knowing. "In any current moment of uncertainty, I think most people think what they want and need is elusive certainty. So this moment actually demands some measure of healthy, humble uncertainty from leaders. Leaders can exemplify mature doubt, centered groundedness and an unwillingness to divide a community along important-but-temporary ideological lines."[8]

The visceral uncertainty that overtakes us in the wilderness is not an injury; it's a healing. It opens up an even deeper exploration of the transformation of heart, of spirit, of soul that is possible only in the wilderness. The further distance we gain in our wanderings, the greater depths we can plumb in our wonderings, too. Maurice Winley testifies, "The journey that God has led me through has been into the wilderness of my own soul. It's prepared me. My work now is to bring others to a place of being able to spot their promise ahead and encourage them to journey with me as they make their way."[9]

No doubt the wilderness's beauty is easier to enjoy from a distance than it is in its midst. It will always be our nature to seek more comfort, a familiar home, the permanent provision of sustenance that out there threatens to slip from between our fingers. For the entire duration of the Israelites' forty years in the desert, they yearned—first for the pyramids they came from and then for the promised land they had not quite reached. They struggled mightily to live in the here-and-now, in the liminality between the two poles of their journey. This, too, is a characteristic of wilderness. We will always want to leave it behind. Like the Israelites, we are likely to trade in our tents for a temple at our first opportunity. But the wilderness is the place of our greatest growth. It's the place where a bigger dream is held and pondered, where the disturbed past crumbles to pieces, where distance offers the possibility of putting all our shattered pieces into a new arrangement, a mosaic treasure. We should not rush to leave the wilderness's wisdom behind.

The refrain for this stage of the Mosaic leadership cycle is "not yet." At first blush, the phrase is reminiscent of a parent's canned response to the backseat inquiry "Are we there yet?" Yet, if we allow ourselves not only to repeat it to others but to internalize it for ourselves, it invites us to hold onto uncertainty just a moment longer and to embrace hope a touch more tightly, even as the road ahead stretches beyond sight.

Are *we* there yet? Not yet. But in our journeying, have we become a broader, more diverse, more empowered mixed multitude? Absolutely.

Are we *there* yet? Not yet. But with each passing day, is "there" coming into greater focus, the contours of promise visible more sharply along the skyline? Most certainly.

Are we there *yet*? Not yet. But as we pick up each sacred shard of our mosaic lives, are we richer in wisdom, more heartfelt in our yearning, more artful about arranging the pieces together into a picture of love and liberation? Yes, yes, we are.

Notes

1 Midrash Petirat Moshe, a midrash that describes the final events leading up to Moses's death, at which God and God's angels are present. The midrash dates between the seventh and eleventh centuries.

2 Simchat Torah is an autumnal holiday that marks the end of the public Torah reading cycle and initiates the beginning of the new one.

3 Eugene Kim, email, March 23, 2023.

4 "In the image of God."

5 Winley, interview.

6 Springer, interview.

7 Luria, interview.

8 Adam Kligfeld, email, March 15, 2023.

9 Winley, interview.

EPILOGUE

Not to make loss beautiful,
But to make loss the place
Where beauty starts. Where
the heart understands
For the first time
The nature of its journey.

. . .

And now loss
Has made us thoughtful.

—GREGORY ORR, "NOT TO MAKE LOSS BEAUTIFUL"

Toward the end of the Israelites' journey, there is in the Exodus text an exhaustive list of building materials for the tabernacle that will more permanently house the most precious articles of their covenant. The list includes an item that at first seems almost inconsequential to the Israelites' progress toward promise: mirrors. "[Moses] made the copper washbasin with its copper stand from the copper mirrors among the ranks of women assigned to the meeting tent's entrance" (Exod 38:8). Nowhere else in the text have we read about the women gathering mirrors before leaving Egypt. Mirrors have no place in the story of wilderness wanderings. Shouldn't these instruments—backwards-facing by nature—have been on the list of things left behind? And yet, near the end of the journey, mirrors show up in the story, and they appear to be a critically important element of the tabernacle's construction.

It was left to the rabbis of later generations to unpack this mystery. One midrash asks:[1] Mirrors? What mirrors? Why, among many references to copper in the tabernacle's materials, is this particular item called out?[2] Perhaps, the rabbis answer, the women had carried mirrors all along. Or maybe, the midrash playfully suggests, the whole exodus journey was in fact a visual trick played on them by mirrors. While the Israelites walked steadily toward a land promised to flow with milk and honey, the answered promise of liberation was first evident in their mirrored reflections. As time and distance separated them from their slavery, the image the Israelites saw reflected back by those polished copper vanities began to resemble an inner freedom. Aviva Zornberg proposes: What if their transformation—represented by the subtle changes in their countenance staring back at them—*is* the promised land they were seeking all along?[3]

If we look closely, we can see in every mirror multiple images. In the foreground, the line of sight lands directly on the one who seeks a genuine self-reflection. But mirrors also allow their holder to see just over their shoulder—to what is behind them, to witness how far they have come. Mirrors catch a glimpse of the footprints we leave behind us, traces of where we've stumbled, what we've learned. And maybe, depending on how we hold the mirror, we might even be able to see where our footprints changed course, where we found a new path forward in the terrain we've left behind.

These pages have told the stories of a number of Mosaic leaders, including Moses himself. Their leadership stories express profound transformation; their personal mirrors reveal both inner and outer shifts. In the distant background of each of their mirrored reflections is the faint outline of a pyramid. It's there in every mirror, but it fades with each step toward liberation. There is also a middle distance in these leaders' hindsight. It's a composite, a gathering of faces. People, not pyramids, a whole company in which power and responsibility are shared, where challenges are met together. In that collective image, in that mosaic of broken pieces picked up and carried, of stories shared and amplified, life finds a new way, as it always does.

In his final moments, as he stood at the edge of the promised land, perhaps Moses, too, paused to look into one of the women's mirrors. He would have seen with his "undimmed eyes and unabated vigor" (Deut 34:7) his own face, weathered by a long journey. His reflection, this leader of the Israelites, was born in empire. It had been broken over a long wilderness. It had been put back together again in a different shape. His wrinkles revealed a surprising refinement. Perhaps, in our midrashic imaginations, before Moses closed his eyes for the final time, he looked back on how far he had come—how far they had all come—and felt a hard-won peace wash over him, gift and reward both.

Qoheleth, the wise and sometimes wry author of Ecclesiastes, writes, "A season is set for everything, a time for every experience under heaven" (Eccl 3:1). The words are just as true spoken somberly between tears at a funeral as they are when harmonized in the joyful song by The Byrds.[4] And, of course, the saying is no less true in the work of leadership.

For every leader, there are seasons of unfettered growth and seasons of profound loss. Seasons of maintaining the status quo and seasons of challenging it with every fiber of our being. Seasons of wholehearted, whole-souled love of the holy work ahead of us and seasons of exhaustion, burnout, and dread for the days to come. This is where leadership lives and where it grows: in a repeated rhythm of disturbing a familiar confinement, distancing from the long-unquestioned story that shaped its borders, and dreaming—again and again—of a promise that has not yet arrived.

Qoheleth catches himself at the edge of melancholy, offering reassurance both to himself and to his readers: "I realized, too, that whatever God has brought to pass will recur evermore. Nothing can be added to it, and nothing taken from it. . . . What is occurring occurred long ago, so, too, what is yet to be. And God picks up the pieces" (Eccl 3:15–16).[5]

This is not the first time that the faithful have faltered or that religion has been reimagined. Our most indestructible objects have broken before; their pieces were carried this far through a long and unformed wilderness. You are called to the great, humbling work of reshaping those pieces and of being reshaped in turn. No matter what season you find yourself in, take heart. The work is not yours alone.

Notes

1 Midrash Tanhuma Pekudei 9.
2 Professor Rachel Andelman proposes that the mirrors were a symbol of transformation, representing the Israelite women's efforts to grow their nation in the early days of their servitude in Egypt. "In the theology of this midrash, God is seen to be on the side of women, with their audacious mission to let 'life find a way,' . . . their significance as icons of vanity is transformed into emblems of resistance, even transformation." Rachel Adelman, "A Copper Laver Made from Women's Mirrors," The Torah, https://tinyurl.com/ywsazw5a, accessed April 2, 2023.
3 Zornberg, *Particulars of Rapture*, 61.
4 "Turn! Turn! Turn!," written by Pete Seeger, 1959, performed by The Byrds.
5 Translation is a blend of JPS and the authors, as well as the poetic interpretation of Calvin G. Seerveld, from his book *God Picks Up the Pieces* (Sioux Center, IA: Dordt Press, 2023). Our gratitude to Craig Mattson for sharing this excellent reference.

Acknowledgments

For each of us, setting out to write a book about an idea we recognized as deeply true but could still barely articulate was like deciding to scale one of those pretty mountains in the Himalayas after a few weekend backpacking trips. We're indebted to the people who caught the thread of what we knew we wanted to say, even before the words came. We are humbled by their vision and their support.

The Lilly Endowment has undergirded our work. We are hugely grateful.

Kenda Creasy Dean, deeply faithful innovator and theologian, understood from the beginning that we hoped to contribute to the current of changemaking that is already washing over the institutions of organized religion, opening space for God's new thing. She is a visionary, a maker of things that work, a dear friend.

Carmelle Beaugelin, research partner extraordinaire, helped ground our thinking in a strand of thought already in process and is among those on whose shoulders this book sits. She also added creative flair to every one of our conversations.

The six leaders profiled in this book have taught us volumes, only a small fraction of which made it into these pages, but all of which has affected us deeply. Rabbi Sara Luria, Reverend Maurice Winley, Reverend Eugene Kim, Rabbi Adam Kligfeld, De'Amon Harges, and Father Richard Springer—you live out a liturgy both poetic and prophetic. Thank you for allowing us to pray with you.

Beth Gaede was the editor at Fortress Press who bravely took a chance on this book even as its outline shape-shifted in front of her. And to be sure, the chance she took was not only on a book but on the two of us. We hope to repay that faith in time, and we remain thoroughly grateful until that day comes. She retired just as our writing began, to our great loss; but Yvonne D. Hawkins ably took her place and has been an invaluable partner and guide ever since.

From Elan

In an ironic twist of fate, writing a book about leadership has helped me see more clearly just how many leadership qualities I lack and, in turn, how heavily I rely on my family, friends, and God as partners. As Kathi and I have emphasized in these pages, leadership is not a solo act, and the wilderness is no place to be ventured alone.

I'm eternally grateful to my mother, Smadar, and my father, Michael *z"l* (of blessed memory), who first modeled for me what a life of loving service looks like. Sometimes it meant giving the *d'var Torah* (short sermon) at our *minyan*, and other times it meant sweeping up the crumbs after *kiddush* lunch. Always it meant treating others with dignity and finding the good in all people. Most of all (as my family can attest), they taught me that opting for the most direct route usually meant missing out on flowers to smell and wonders to behold, so one should try to take the circuitous, slow road whenever possible. And to my sister, Talia, and brother, Dan, thank you for walking those patient paths with me all these years later.

To my wife, Lizzie, whose encouragement buoyed me when the writing process threatened to sink my spirits and whose generous leadership wisdom fills each of these pages—the white space between the black ink.

To Micah, the earliest reader of these words and the most proud supporter of my tireless efforts to write them. To Nessa, who constantly reminds me to savor the sunset as our days fade away. To Ayla, who knew exactly when I needed to be lifted up after long days of writing and demanded countless family dance parties to remedy the situation.

In addition to being raised by and loved by some of the greats, I am also blessed to stand among giants each day at work, too. Rabbi Irwin Kula took one of the great chances of his career by hiring me and, as is the tradition at Clal, invited me to leave my role in the pulpit and take a one-year position with him. That was many, many one-year positions ago. Rabbi Brad Hirschfield taught me a lesson I will never forget. I came to him after what I felt was a devastating failure of my rabbinic leadership. He taught me then and models for me now that the broken pieces of the tablets sat next to the whole ones in the ark of the covenant—two treasures side by side. And Dr. Jack McGourty, whose generosity of spirit, wisdom, and trust knows no bounds.

My work would not be possible without the steadfast support and mentorship that Clal's board has given to me over the years. Among so many others, Richie Pearlstone has been a generous friend, a profoundly humble supporter, and—always—a fearless visionary. Erin Satterwhite believes in my leadership more than I do, and she has taught me unforgettable lessons about leading with integrity and humanity, not just by sharing ideas with me but by modeling it each and every day of her life. Rachel Littman took a tremendous leap of faith—on me, on accepting a board role with an organization she knew precious little about, and on the radical idea that Jewish wisdom has the potential to serve anyone, anywhere.

In Pirkei Avot (Ethics of our Ancestors), an Jewish ethical guidebook of sorts, Joshua ben Perahiah teaches, "Find yourself a rabbi, and acquire for yourself a friend. And judge all others with the scale weighted in their favor" (Pirkei Avot 1:6). I am blessed to have two mentors in Rabbi Cheryl Peretz and Rabbi Wayne Franklin, who started out as my rabbis, emerged as dear, precious friends, and even in my most challenging moments judge me with overwhelming merit. I will forever be grateful for their teaching, their friendship, and their generosity.

Writing this book has been a labor not only of my own love but also of the love that my team at Glean Network has for our ambitious mission. As I stepped back to write this book over the last year, they poured that love into the many places and spaces that I had previously occupied in our work and far exceeded any successes I had achieved beforehand. To Sandy Hong, Minahil Khan, and Rodney Eric Lopez: I could not possibly feel more grateful to be your fellow traveler in our holy work.

Last, I am blessed by the love of friends who know me as I am, love me in spite of it, and always pick up the phone when I call. To my soul brother Rabbi David Singer, who knew instinctively that I needed a couple of days away in the midst of writing this and hopped on a flight to meet me (twice and counting). To my confidante and companion Adam Tilove, whose infectious joy and bountiful cheerleading kept me fueled throughout this project. And to the inimitable Kevin Blake, with whom I took the same three-mile walk around Providence countless times, whose wry humor, steady insight, and genuine care always served to buoy my spirits.

From Kathi

All changemaking begins with a small and tentative idea. It's the people who surround the idea maker, in the way they receive and reinforce and refine an initial thought, that makes the difference between an imagining that grows into something solid and the millions of other good ideas that get abandoned before they hit the ground. The wonderings that became the

Changemaker Initiative got clearer and stronger over countless conversations with Julien Phillips, Erika Gregory, Jay Johnson, Brian McLaren, Daniel Pryfogle, Susan Beaumont, and Gil Rendle, whose curiosity, intellect, and hope have inspired me again and again. I'm so grateful.

Anne Evans and Vipin Thekk courageously and open-heartedly shared Ashoka's learned wisdom as we began to reimagine Christian discipleship as "becoming compassion-driven changemakers like Jesus."

The Lilly Endowment's investment in the Changemaker Initiative has made all the difference. Lilly and the visionary people such as Chanon Ross who lead from there are doing the extravagantly generous and often unseen work of lifting up hopeful experiments like this one. Their partnership is opening a way for all of us who know that the church we have loved must change.

In the five years I spent with them, the people and community of Los Altos United Methodist Church in Silicon Valley were graciously, bravely, and surprisingly ready to risk something big for something good. We gathered our stories together and made that church feel like a place where truly anything was possible. I'm especially grateful to the intrepid Changemaker leadership team, Kim Jones, Karen Kehlet, Yvonne Murray, Melissa Allison, and Lisa Conover Hustis; to the team of gifted pastors and ministry directors I was privileged to work with, Dirk Damonte, Sam Blewis, Jeong Park, Siteri Maravou, Carol Damonte, and Jeremy Steele; and to my always-partners in leading change, Denise Robinson and Ken Greathouse.

I have no doubt that my path to belief in a God who makes the universe a place of flourishing was carved out by the unconditional love I have always felt from my parents. My father, Greg Tcherkoyan, died in the year we were writing this book. My dad was always the first to stand up and applaud whatever I wanted to venture into next, whether he understood it completely or not. He did the same with this book; I hope that somehow he can see it as it comes to fruition. My mom, Seta, is the touchstone I reach for regularly to restore my faith in the plain truth of kindness and love.

My sisters grew up in the same family of generosity and warmth. They, too, bring those qualities to every interaction. My elegant sister Patti, my farm-life partner and sister Kirsti—they make life fun and full.

And Stacey, daughter toward whom my heart is always leaning. You, too, are a changemaker in so many ways. My thumb is always pointing up for you as yours has always been for me.